How We Talk to Each Other - The Messages We Send With Our Words and Body Language

Ulf Lubienetzki · Heidrun Schüler-Lubienetzki

How We Talk to Each Other - The Messages We Send With Our Words and Body Language

Psychology of Human Communication

Ulf Lubienetzki
entwicklung GbR
Hamburg, Germany

Heidrun Schüler-Lubienetzki
entwicklung GbR
Hamburg, Germany

This book is a translation of the original German edition „Was wir uns wie sagen und zeigen" by Lubienetzki, Ulf, published by Springer-Verlag GmbH, DE in 2020. The translation was done with the help of artificial intelligence (machine translation by the service DeepL.com). A subsequent human revision was done primarily in terms of content, so that the book will read stylistically differently from a conventional translation. Springer Nature works continuously to further the development of tools for the production of books and on the related technologies to support the authors.

ISBN 978-3-662-64436-2   ISBN 978-3-662-64437-9   (eBook)
https://doi.org/10.1007/978-3-662-64437-9

© Springer-Verlag GmbH Germany, part of Springer Nature 2022
This work is subject to copyright. All rights are reserved by the Publisher, whether the whole or part of the material is concerned, specifically the rights of reprinting, reuse of illustrations, recitation, broadcasting, reproduction on microfilms or in any other physical way, and transmission or information storage and retrieval, electronic adaptation, computer software, or by similar or dissimilar methodology now known or hereafter developed.
The use of general descriptive names, registered names, trademarks, service marks, etc. in this publication does not imply, even in the absence of a specific statement, that such names are exempt from the relevant protective laws and regulations and therefore free for general use.
The publisher, the authors and the editors are safe to assume that the advice and information in this book are believed to be true and accurate at the date of publication. Neither the publisher nor the authors or the editors give a warranty, expressed or implied, with respect to the material contained herein or for any errors or omissions that may have been made. The publisher remains neutral with regard to jurisdictional claims in published maps and institutional affiliations.

This Springer imprint is published by the registered company Springer-Verlag GmbH, DE part of Springer Nature.
The registered company address is: Heidelberger Platz 3, 14197 Berlin, Germany

Foreword

*This book is a translation of the original German edition „Was wir uns wie sagen und zeigen" by Lubienetzki, Ulf **and Schüler-Lubienetzki**, Heidrun, published by Springer-Verlag GmbH.*

For more than two decades we have been dealing professionally with human communication. Whether as coaches, trainers, consultants or even as managers, for us it has always been about exchanging factual information, communicating personal perceptions and feelings, evaluating something or even someone, or even achieving something together with one or more people. Over time, we have gathered a lot of our own experience in communication and have developed our knowledge in a targeted manner. An important part of our work is passing on our experience and knowledge to other people. In our profession, this is mostly done in the form of seminars and training sessions. The great advantage of seminars and training sessions, be it face to face or online, is that it is possible to specifically address the individual questions and needs of the participants. Therefore, the most important component of our events is always the work on case studies that participants bring with them, as well as the development and testing of solutions. Inevitably, the possibilities of reaching people with seminars on communication topics are limited. The cooperation with various universities as well as with Springer Verlag offers us the opportunity to reach significantly more people. We were and are aware that it is in the nature of publications not to be able to respond directly to individual questions and examples from readers. We have therefore seen it as our essential task to convey the knowledge we have compiled on various communication topics as clearly and as closely as possible to what is possible in seminars and training sessions. Three essential elements shape our textbooks for this purpose:

- An engaging and pleasant-to-read writing style. Textbooks impart knowledge. Putting this knowledge into words in such a way that readers enjoy was our first goal.
- Vividly developed case studies. The core of the knowledge to be conveyed is to the point in the textbook. Our case studies, which often make you smile or even laugh, direct the focus by translating abstract knowledge into comprehensible action in everyday situations.
- Immediate reflection on what has been learned. Communication is an everyday thing. This means that communication is basically accessible to everyone at all times. In the course of reading our textbooks, we specifically encourage readers to experience and try out what they have just read in their own environment.

We hope you'll find our book both interesting and beneficial.

Ulf Lubienetzki
Hamburg, Germany

Heidrun Schüler-Lubienetzki
Hamburg, Germany
May 2020

Contents

1	Introduction	1
2	**Verbal and Non-verbal Communication**	5
2.1	"One Cannot Not Communicate!": A First Look at Communication	8
2.2	The Shannon-Weaver Model	10
2.3	Extended Communication Model According to Watzlawick et al.	12
2.4	Transactional Analysis: The Answer to the Question of Why?	16
2.4.1	The Ego States: A Model of the Structure of the Human Personality	17
2.4.2	Transactions: What Happens Between People	21
2.4.3	People's Views of Life	26
2.5	Communication According to Schulz von Thun	28
2.5.1	The Four Sides of a Message	28
2.5.2	Congruent and Incongruent Communication	30
2.5.3	Communication: It's a Give and Take	31
2.6	Constructivist Perspective on Communication	33
	Literature	34
3	**Communication Styles and Patterns**	37
3.1	Eight Communication Styles According to Schulz von Thun	38
3.2	Tools and Instruments for the Study of Communication	43
3.2.1	(Vicious) Circles in Communication	44
3.2.2	Values and Development Square	47
3.2.3	The Drama Triangle	50
	Literature	55
4	**Disturbed Communication**	57
4.1	Communication Problems	58
4.2	The 12 Communication Roadblocks According to Thomas Gordon	61
	Literature	64
5	**Self-Perception and Perception of Others**	65
	Literature	68
6	**Overall Summary in Keywords**	69
	Supplementary Information	
	Glossary	74
	Index	77

About the Authors

Ulf Lubienetzki

has been working for several years as a consultant, business coach and trainer with specialists and managers in various industries. In addition, he has more than 20 years of experience as a manager up to the executive level in various national and international management consulting firms. Ulf Lubienetzki holds a degree in engineering and has studied social pedagogy and sociology. In the guidebooks and textbooks he has written, he brings his wide-ranging practical experience from working with his clients to bear.

Heidrun Schüler-Lubienetzki

has been working as a business coach, leadership trainer, management consultant and facilitator for more than two decades. Heidrun Schüler-Lubienetzki is a psychologist, with a focus on personnel and organizational development, as well as a talk therapist. In more than two decades, she has worked with several thousand specialists and executives up to board level. As an author of guidebooks as well as specialist books and textbooks, she passes on her knowledge and experience.

Both authors lead together the company entwicklung GbR in their coaching house in Hamburg-Rahlstedt. entwicklung GbR stands for

- Coaching of specialists and managers
- Individual and team training
- Consulting for change processes in organizations

Together with its clients, entwicklung GbR works to maintain and increase the personal performance of specialists and managers, to develop high-performance teams, to reduce the waste of resources caused by dysfunctional conflicts, and to provide competent advice and goal-oriented support for change.

If you have any questions or need information about personal coaching, seminars or training, you will find a wide range of information at ▶ http://www.entwicklung-hamburg.de

If you have any questions, feedback or suggestions, please do not hesitate to contact us by e-mail: info@entwicklung-hamburg.de

Introduction

The explanations in this chapter are based on the following study brief: Lubienetzki, U. and Schüler-Lubienetzki, H. (2016). WHAT WE SAY AND SHOW EACH OTHER AND HOW. HUMAN COMMUNICATION. Study letter of the Fresenius University of Applied Sciences (Hochschule Fresenius) online plus GmbH. Idstein: Hochschule Fresenius online plus GmbH.

© Springer-Verlag GmbH Germany, part of Springer Nature 2022
U. Lubienetzki, H. Schüler-Lubienetzki, *How We Talk to Each Other - The Messages We Send With Our Words and Body Language*, https://doi.org/10.1007/978-3-662-64437-9_1

When people meet, they interact and communicate. This is inevitable and applies in both private and professional contexts. In this book, we have compiled for you what we consider to be the relevant fundamentals of human communication. Some of these basic insights were developed 50–60 years ago and still set the standard today when it comes to issues of human communication. Therefore, the books by Paul Watzlawick and Friedemann Schulz von Thun have retained their relevance and are still high on the sales lists.

We do not think about many things in everyday life, we just do them. If we take a closer look, humans have a deep need to communicate about communication. Therefore, there are many adages and proverbs about the way another person speaks and behaves (e.g., "It's not what you do, but the way that you do it."). It is also commonplace to analyse the communication of others. This can be seen, for example, in remarks such as "She looks sad.", "His voice was trembling with anger." or "She was not happy about the present at all!".

In this book, we would like to provide you with a repertoire of concepts and models with which you can think about communication in a structured way and exchange ideas. At the same time, this book is communication itself. We convey factual content on the subject of communication to you via the text and at one point or another you may also learn something about us and our personal experiences between the lines.

On your way through this book, you will encounter the axioms of human communication and what follows from them. You will learn about different perspectives on communication and different communication styles and patterns. You will learn what it means to communicate successfully and what makes it challenging, difficult and even impossible to communicate successfully. All this helps to observe and analyse communication and to derive starting points for behavioural changes. And you will learn, almost in passing, to have a better understanding of yourself and how you communicate.

We try and hope to succeeded to communicate with you in an accessible way in this book. In addition to the theory, you will find many examples from the world of Construction Machines Smith Ltd that will help you to understand the contents. At one point or another, you will certainly recognise people from your environment or even yourself. You will also certainly find various examples amusing, which we have deliberately exaggerated to illustrate a connection. Of course, all this is no coincidence. It shows us that the concepts and models for communication on which the examples are based work in everyday life.

Throughout more than two decades of professional activity, we have experienced that deeper knowledge of communicative processes is beneficial and relevant. Reflecting on our communication and observing the communication of others gives us many clues on how to communicate in a targeted and successful way. Misunderstandings, conflicts and ambiguities cost time and nerves. Appreciative and trusting interaction, on the other hand, helps to avoid such developments or at least offers the chance of solutions. Unfortunately, we cannot offer recipes that always succeed. People and the world are too complex for that. But at least we can significantly increase the probability that communication will succeed.

Introduction

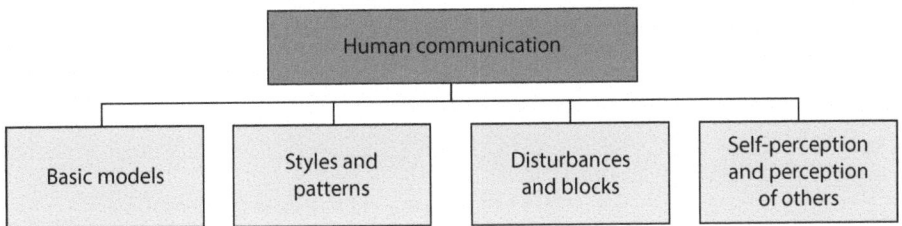

Fig. 1.1 The book at a glance

Figure 1.1 shows you the structure of this book at a glance.

This book is divided into five chapters. After this first introductory chapter, we will get into ▶ Chap. 2 with the basic models of human communication. Then, in ▶ Chap. 3, we will look at communication styles and patterns. In ▶ Chap. 4, we will take a closer look at communication breakdowns and blocks and conclude in ▶ Chap. 5 with self-perception and perception of others.

Verbal and Non-verbal Communication

Basic Concepts and Models

Contents

2.1 "One Cannot Not Communicate!": A First Look at Communication – 8

2.2 The Shannon-Weaver Model – 10

2.3 Extended Communication Model According to Watzlawick et al. – 12

2.4 Transactional Analysis: The Answer to the Question of Why? – 16

The explanations in this chapter are based on the following study brief: Lubienetzki, U. and Schüler-Lubienetzki, H. (2016). WHAT WE SAY AND SHOW EACH OTHER AND HOW. HUMAN COMMUNICATION. Study letter of the Fresenius University of Applied Sciences (Hochschule Fresenius) online plus GmbH. Idstein: Hochschule Fresenius online plus GmbH.

© Springer-Verlag GmbH Germany, part of Springer Nature 2022
U. Lubienetzki, H. Schüler-Lubienetzki, *How We Talk to Each Other - The Messages We Send With Our Words and Body Language*, https://doi.org/10.1007/978-3-662-64437-9_2

- 2.4.1 The Ego States: A Model of the Structure of the Human Personality – 17
- 2.4.2 Transactions: What Happens Between People – 21
- 2.4.3 People's Views of Life – 26

2.5 Communication According to Schulz von Thun – 28
- 2.5.1 The Four Sides of a Message – 28
- 2.5.2 Congruent and Incongruent Communication – 30
- 2.5.3 Communication: It's a Give and Take – 31

2.6 Constructivist Perspective on Communication – 33

Literature – 34

Verbal and Non-verbal Communication

Human communication is sometimes quite miraculous. We are often surprised when seemingly simple human encounters escalate unpredictably or when situations that seem complex at first glance suddenly resolve themselves. We want to understand what is behind this and how we can harness this knowledge to improve our communication. You will receive the tools needed for communication about communication on the following pages.

After reading this chapter in-depth, you will be able to …
- Define **human communication** and describe and analyse it using different approaches and models.
- Reproduce and explain the five **axioms** of human communication according to Watzlawick, Beavin and Jackson (1968).
- Differentiate the **four sides of a message** in the sense of Schulz von Thun (2013).
- Recognise connections in conversations from the perspective of **transactional analysis** according to Eric Berne (1961) and assess them in terms of **transactions** and **ego states** of the participants.
- Explain how **life views** or **incongruent messages** can influence the success of communication.
- Present the **constructivist view** of communication.

We live in the age of information and communication. At least theoretically we could communicate at any time from any place on earth with any other person in any other place. The communication possibilities in today's world are already impressive, especially if we still remember (or our parents' generation tells us about) the age when telephones still had a cord and a rotary dial. In this book, however, we are less interested in the amount we communicate and more in what communication actually is (▶ Excursus: Origin of the Term Communication) and how we can describe it and look at it more closely. Only when the essence of communication is accessible to us can we analyse communication and ultimately further develop it.

Important
Of course, we can study communication from different points of view and with different goals. In this book, we are mainly concerned with making communication successful. In doing so, we assume that communication is goal-oriented and that the success of communication results from the fact that the respective goal of communication is achieved.

Excursus: Origin of the Term Communication

The term *communication* is derived from the Latin verb *communicare* and means, among other things, "the process by which messages or information is sent from one place or person to another" and "also the exchange of information and the expression of feeling that can result in understanding" (Cambridge University Press, n.d.-b).

2.1 "One Cannot Not Communicate!": A First Look at Communication

> **Definition**
>
> **Human communication** is the verbal or nonverbal interaction between at least two people (Schulz von Thun, 2013; Watzlawick et al., 1968).

In addition to this definition of human communication, we would like to say at the outset: People who meet also communicate (Watzlawick et al., 1968). Perhaps you are now wondering whether this apodictic (i.e. considered incontrovertible) statement can be true. Fortunately, you are a human being and can test the truth of this statement out on yourself.

▶ **Example: Wordless Communication**

How about you try not to communicate with another person you meet? Here is a suggestion for an experiment:

Someone enters the room you are in (e.g. a colleague, a friend or a complete stranger) and you deliberately do not communicate. For example, you could try it like this: You deliberately do not look at the other person, naturally do not speak a word to them and do not react to them in any other way. Another, perhaps simpler option would be to just leave the room without a word. You may think of other variations.

Before you actually start the self-experiment and unintentionally cause something unexpected to happen, please change your perspective for a moment:

Now, you enter a room and perceive a person in this room. The person looks away or even walks away, if you address them, they do not respond and do not react to you in any other way. What message do you receive? Has the person actually not communicated with you? At the very least, the person's behaviour shows that they do not want to communicate with you. Depending on the relationship you have with the other person, you may wonder what the unwillingness to communicate is about or even make assumptions about it. "Is the other person mad at me?", "Does she/he not like me?": You may ask yourself these and similar questions.

You see: Even a person who does not speak or otherwise respond is very much communicating. Even two complete strangers who, for example, meet in a queue and look past each other or turn their backs on each other could, for example, send out the message "I do not want to communicate (with you)". ◀

Watzlawick et al. (1968) have formulated their first **axiom** "One cannot *not* communicate" (p. 51) for the communication situation presented in the example.

▸ **Important**

The communication model of Watzlawick, Beavin, and Jackson is presented in more detail in ▶ Sect. 2.3. Here you can get an initial overview.

2.1 · "One Cannot Not Communicate!": A First Look...

> **Definition**
>
> An **axiom** is "a statement or principle that is generally accepted to be true" and might also be "a formal statement or principle in mathematics, science, etc., from which others statements can be obtained" (Cambridge University Press, n.d.-a).

Their train of thought on this, described in their book "Pragmatics of Human Communication" (Watzlawick et al., 1968), begins with the fact that every living being, including every human being, behaves in some way at every point in its life. Human behaviour is a basic trait that is always there. You can try another self experiment if you like, or take our word for it: you always behave somehow. Watzlawick et al. (1968) express this fact very simply: "one cannot *not* behave" (p. 48).

The next step in their thinking is that behaviour in an interpersonal encounter always has a communicative character. This is true even if the behaviour actually has nothing to do with other people, for example, because we have not yet perceived them at all. As soon as another person perceives us, they will interpret our behaviour in some way. The other person translates our behaviour into a statement or a message. How others interpret the message depends on many factors.

> ▶ **Example: Interpretation of Wordless Communication**
>
> Let us stick with the previous example:
>
> You enter a room where there is another person. This other person does not respond to you. You may interpret this behaviour as "I did not notice you."
>
> Another interpretation might be, "I'm ignoring you and want to be left alone." Many other interpretations are possible here and how you interpret the message depends on your relationship with that person.
>
> If the person is a close friend, you are more likely to interpret the behaviour as, "Oh, he/she didn't see me." If there is a conflict or argument with the person, the message could also be "I'm ignoring you. Leave me alone!". ◀

Environmental factors also influence the subjective interpretation of one person's behaviour by another: Is it noisy or quiet, light or dark, are there one or more people in the room, and, and ... the list is probably endless.

If - as explained - human behaviour always has a communicative character (in other words, it is communication), the axiom mentioned at the beginning "One cannot *not* communicate" follows directly from the sentence "One cannot *not* behave" (Watzlawick et al., 1968, pp. 48–51).

> ❓ **Reflection task: How do I behave?**
>
> You have just learned that an axiom is a statement generally considered to be true. So what prevents you from checking the validity of the first axiom according to Watzlawick et al. for yourself? Find a convenient opportunity, e.g. in a professional context or privately with friends, in which you consciously observe your behaviour. Please ask yourself how the people around you perceive your behaviour and what messages people might receive from it. With people familiar to you, you could even go a step further and, following your analysis, ask them about their perception and evaluation.

> **Important**
>
> Let us summarise: Communication also takes place through behaviour. How you behave is interpreted by other people. However, the result of the interpretation is very subjective and depends on many factors. The most important ones are the person themselves as well as the relationship between the communicating people. Environmental factors also impact on the process of interpretation (Schulz von Thun, 2013; Watzlawick et al., 1968).

We will go into more detail later on how personal disposition, as well as the relationship between people, affects communication.

From the simple examples in this section, we can observe how quickly things become complicated when we think about or communicate about human communication. That is why we need a common language to describe communication itself and what happens in communication. Models reduce complexity and make a common set of signs available to communicate about communication. Watzlawick et al. or Schulz von Thun use the term **metacommunication** in this context.

Definition

Metacommunication is a conceptual system and framework to communicate about communication (Schulz von Thun, 2013, pp. 101–106; Watzlawick et al., 1968, p. 40).

Each of the communication models presented below has its justification. There is no right or wrong, but the question in each case is: What aspect of communication is up for debate and which of the models is most suitable for describing and analysing this aspect?

2.2 The Shannon-Weaver Model

A simple model of communication comes from Claude E. Shannon and Warren Weaver (1972). It is often called the **sender-receiver model**. ◘ Figure 2.1 gives you an overview of the model.

The model shows that communication takes place between (at least) one sender and (at least) one receiver in a specific or defined situational context. Encoded messages (e.g. speech) are exchanged between sender and receiver. According to this model, a prerequisite for successful communication is that the sender(s) and the receiver(s) have a common set of signs available for encoding and decoding the exchanged messages (Shannon & Weaver, 1972).

2.2 · The Shannon-Weaver Model

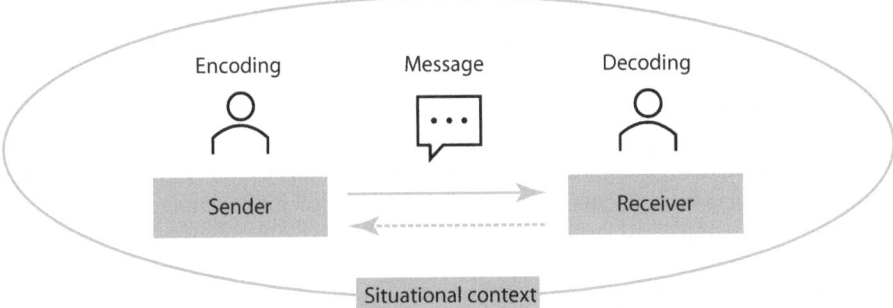

Fig. 2.1 Sender-receiver model according to Shannon & Weaver. According to Shannon and Weaver, communication always takes place between at least one sender and at least one receiver and always in a specific context. Messages are transmitted in encoded form and must be decoded by the respective receiver. (Source: Own representation based on Shannon and Weaver, 1972, p. 7)

> ► Example: Message Decryption
>
> You are in China for the first time and cannot speak or understand Mandarin. You will have very limited ability to exchange verbally coded messages with a local in the Chinese province.
>
> Holidaymakers in foreign countries whose language they neither speak nor understand are familiar with such situations. Tourists often rely on non-verbal encoding. Literally "with hands and feet," they send messages which are to be decoded by the receiver who, in turn, answers with an encoded message. Complex issues can be conveyed rather laboriously in this way, but simple messages - for example, the purchase of a souvenir - can usually be exchanged successfully. ◄

The most important form of encoding messages is a language with its **syntax**. In language, letters are combined to form words and these are combined to form sentences. The words and phrases have **semantics**.

> **Definition**
>
> **Syntax** is "the way in which linguistic elements (such as words) are put together to form constituents (such as phrases or clauses)" (Merriam-Webster, n.d.).
>
> The Oxford University Press (n.d.) defines the term **semantics** as "the study of the meanings of words and phrases".

In this context, it is interesting to note that semantics do not necessarily have to be unambiguous and are often only revealed by the context in which they are communicated.

Case Study

If John Smith (you remember: The managing director of Construction Machines Smith Ltd) says the sentence "It's hot." to his wife Anna, in the sauna it could mean that John Smith will leave the sauna shortly or that he wishes the temperature to be reduced. If he says this sentence on a sunlit terrace, he could mean that he would like a parasol. At the doctor's, he might say this phrase to indicate that he may have a fever. You see: Depending on the context, even a simple sentence like this can have very different meanings. ◄

The Shannon-Weaver model is useful to study verbal communication and disorders based on the different understanding of language. The model reaches its limits when communication - as postulated by Watzlawick et al. (1968) - also includes conscious and unconscious human behaviour. So let us look below at an extended model based on the findings of Watzlawick et al.

2.3 Extended Communication Model According to Watzlawick et al.

Two people who speak the same language and have the same vocabulary can, but do not necessarily, communicate successfully. Public political debate, for example, shows us every day that communication is more than the mere exchange of verbal and non-verbal signals. Therefore, the "simple" sender-receiver model can be extended based on the principles of metacommunication developed by Watzlawick et al. (1968, see ◘ Fig. 2.2).

Also, in the extended communication model, at least two people are involved and interaction takes place between the two people. In other words, those involved in the communication process act and react, influencing each other with and in their interactions. The whole thing takes place in an environment or context. At

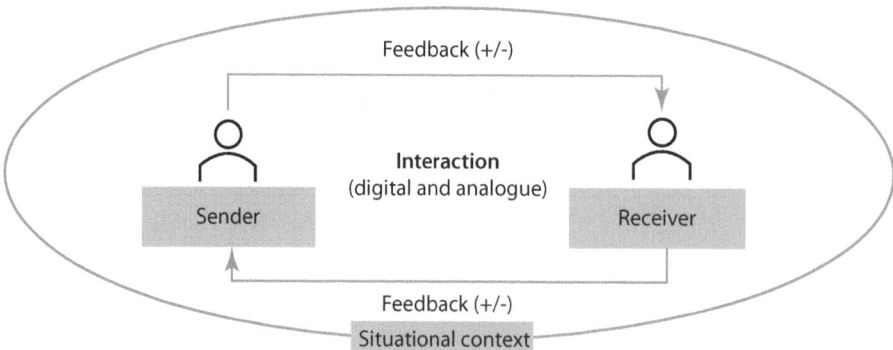

◘ **Fig. 2.2** Extended communication model based on the axioms of Watzlawick et al. Watzlawick et al. have extended the "simple" sender-receiver model. Sender and receiver do not only exchange and decode messages, they influence each other in their interaction. (Source: Own representation based on Watzlawick et al., 1968)

2.3 · Extended Communication Model According to Watzlawick et al.

first glance, the differences to the sender-receiver model are still rather minor. The model only acquires its significantly expanded meaning when the axioms and conclusions postulated by Watzlawick et al. (1968) are incorporated.

We have already met the first **axiom**: "One cannot *not* communicate" (Watzlawick et al., 1968, p. 51).

For the model, this axiom means that communication is continuous. The participants express themselves verbally and/or non-verbally and behave in the communication process without interruption. Through this, the communication participants influence each other at every moment. Communication is always cause and effect; it is, therefore, circular (Watzlawick et al., 1968).

> ► Example: Relationship Determines Factual Content
> In our example of a person meeting another person in a room and remaining silent, it makes a fundamental difference whether strangers, competitors or friends meet. The relationship determines the message of silence in this case. ◄

The second **axiom** formulated by Watzlawick et al. (1968) in this regard is: "Every communication has a content and a relationship aspect such that the latter classifies the former [...]" (p. 54).

This axiom posits the relationship between two people as determining their communication. The meaning of sentences like "You look good today" can range from the highest praise to the deepest insult through the relationship between two people.

> ► Case Study
> John Smith says the sentence "You look good today." to his wife. Since both are very appreciative of each other, she will probably smile and reply with the sentence "Thank you for the compliment."
>
> The other day he wanted to compliment his secretary. To the sentence, "You look good today." he received the angry reply, "Oh, really? And what about all the other days?" ◄

The relationship between two people is so important that when relationships are unresolved, people feel the need to clarify them - either explicitly by asking appropriate questions or implicitly through the way they communicate (Schulz von Thun, 2013; Watzlawick et al., 1968).

> ❓ **Reflection task: Relationship-dependent communication**
> How the relationship between people affects their communication becomes particularly clear in the course of time of a relationship. Please think of your relationship with a person who is very familiar to you today. Please think back to the beginning of your relationship. What was different in your communication with each other compared to today?

When the mutual influence of people on each other and their relationship with each other are of such great importance, it does not make sense to look at communication in isolation, i.e. to focus only on a single person. Communication always involves at least two people and everything that happens involves everyone. Statements and behaviours only acquire meaning when they are placed in the communicative context (Schulz von Thun, 2013; Watzlawick et al., 1968).

> ► Example: Context Analysis
>
> We might condemn a person and judge their behaviour as inadequate at the very moment they yell in a rage at a meeting, bang on the table, and then leave the room. "How childish! No adult behaves like that!", witnesses of the outburst of rage might think at that moment.
>
> We might see the behaviour in a completely different light if we had entered the room a few minutes earlier. If we had entered the room earlier, we would have been able to take into account the fact that the other participants in the meeting had been deliberately and deeply insulting this angry person for at least half an hour in a calm, composed voice and with a friendly expression. They have not refrained from doing so even after his repeated requests for objectivity as well as for moderation. At this moment, an observer might also conclude, "Remarkable how long he has remained calm."
>
> Let's enter the session even earlier: Our initially angry person is not angry at all at this point. On the contrary - with a breathtaking calmness and arrogance he makes personal reproaches to the other meeting participants which are obviously lies. The participants of the meeting, who at first answer calmly and objectively, are driven mad by his lies and his condescending manner. In the end, they knew no other way to help themselves than to hurl savage insults. Wouldn't a viewer now perhaps come to the conclusion that he got what he deserved at the end of the session?
>
> I wonder what else happened in the meeting that we don't know yet? And in the run-up to the meeting? And so on … ◄

Figuratively speaking, communication is circular, that is, without beginning and end. People who are in a relationship with each other communicate and everything that has happened in the relationship so far is part of it. Nevertheless, people set their starting points in communication, which then affect their communicative behaviour. (Schulz von Thun, 2013; Watzlawick et al., 1968).

The corresponding **axiom** to this is: "The nature of a relationship is contingent upon the punctuation of the communicational sequences between the communicants" (Watzlawick et al., 1968, p. 59).

From the preceding example, we can see that we understand those involved differently, depending on where we set the starting point.

The same happens within the communication process. The partners set their starting point. If the starting points deviate from each other, irritations and disturbances can occur.

You can find out more about the circularity of communication and the "vicious circle" that may result from this in ► Sect. 3.2.1.

? Reflection task: actions and reactions

Is there a person with whom you have frequent contact and whom you do not particularly like? If there is no such person, please think of a public person, e.g. a politician, who makes you feel uncomfortable. Now, please think back to the last time you

2.3 · Extended Communication Model According to Watzlawick et al.

met this person, or in the case of public figures, the last time you experienced them. What did this person say in that particular instance and what did this statement trigger in you? What did your reaction refer to? Was it actually just what was said at that moment or were you reacting to what was said in context to previous statements? Was what was said at that moment perhaps even reasonable, but you could not acknowledge it because of the statements made in the past?

The ways in which actors interact are referred to by Watzlawick et al. (1968) as *modalities*. The **axiom** for this is stated as follows: "Human beings communicate both digitally and analogically" (Watzlawick et al., 1968, p. 66).

The **digital modality** (language, signs, symbols, etc.) is primarily used to communicate factual content. This modality is not very accessible for relationships and feelings (Watzlawick et al., 1968).

► Example: Modalities

Many words are necessary to express how much you love another person. A loving hug expresses this feeling instantly, sophisticatedly and without words. ◄

The level of the relationship is illuminated via the **analogic modality** (facial expressions, gestures, behaviour, etc.). As precise as digital expressions are (e.g. in the form of linguistic expressions), analogic ones are equally imprecise. Most of the time, these are ambiguous. A smile can express kindness or contempt. There are tears of joy and sadness. There is no complete certainty in communication that messages will reach the other person. However, by combining digital and analogic modalities, the intended message can be made clear. The overall picture emerges on all channels (Schulz von Thun, 2013; Watzlawick et al., 1968).

Every person is individual and has their personality, their views, their values and principles, their own experiences and much more. This individuality also determines the course of communication, the definition of the relationship as well as the expectations of the other communication participants (Schulz von Thun, 2013; Watzlawick et al., 1968).

The fifth and final **axiom** of Watzlawick et al. (1968) is: "All communicational interchanges are either symmetrical or complementary, depending on whether they are based on equality or difference" (p. 70).

Communication is decisively influenced by how the partners define their relationship with each other at every moment of the communication process. If the communication is *symmetrical,* this means that both communication partners strive for equality and interact accordingly. They behave as mirror images of each other, so to speak. Strength is mirrored with strength, weakness is mirrored with weakness, or hardness is mirrored with hardness, etc. *Complementary communication* shows a matching difference in behaviour. It is not a matter of up and down, strong and weak, or good and bad, but of matching and expected difference. Such complementary relationships occur between teachers and students, mother and child, or managers and employees, etc. What the expectations are in such relationships depends, among other things, on the cultural background. If the expectations of complementarity are not met, communication breakdowns occur. For example, if an older person in Japan is not treated with a certain respect by a younger person, this circumstance can significantly impair communication or even make it impossible. The communication partners simply do not understand each other.

It follows that: Regardless of whether the communication situation is symmetrical or complementary, it is crucial for the course of communication whether the partners have the same or a different definition of their relationship. Deviations in the definition can lead to disruptions (Schulz von Thun, 2013; Watzlawick et al., 1968).

> **Important**
> In addition to the five axioms, the book "Pragmatics of Human Communication – A Study of Interactional Patterns, Pathologies, and Paradoxes" by Watzlawick et al. (1968) contains many in-depth aspects of human communication. To deepen the topic, it is worth reading even 50 years after the first publication of the book.

2.4 Transactional Analysis: The Answer to the Question of Why?

Watzlawick et al. provide us with a basic framework and "construction kit", so to speak, for talking about communication. We can use it to "hover" over the communication situation from a bird's eye view in order to observe and describe it. We see what is happening between the communication partners and can classify this behaviour. Disturbances in communication also become visible. However, the participants themselves remain a black box in the communication model. Would it not be great if we could describe and examine not only the interactions between the participants but also to some extent what is going on inside the participants? The question "Why do people behave in a certain way in communication processes?" is of particular interest to us. After all, the answer to this question opens up the opportunity for us to change communication between people in a targeted way.

One way of analysing the behaviour of communication participants is the **transactional analysis** (Berne, 1961), which was developed by Eric Berne in the early 1960s as a method of psychotherapy and can also be used beyond psychotherapy.

Note
"A note from our side: We often use the tools of transactional analysis in the coaching process of individuals and teams. In our experience, communication processes and especially communication disorders become very vivid and so explainable with transactional analysis. Through the understanding of what happens in communication and why it happens, it becomes possible to find personal solutions to deal with each other better and more trouble-free in the future."
Ulf Lubienetzki and Heidrun Schüler-Lubienetzki
Authors of the book

> **Important**
> We would like to point out at this point that in this book we only pick out and present select parts of transactional analysis which are fundamentally suitable for examining conversation and group situations and creating possibilities for action for those involved. For a more in-depth study of the topic, we recommend reading Berne (1961).

2.4 · Transactional Analysis: The Answer to the Question of Why?

According to Berne, when people interact with each other, this interaction consists of at least two **transactions**.

> **Definition**
> A **transaction** is "the unit of social intercourse" (Berne, 1966, p. 29).

In this context, Berne speaks of a *transactional stimulus* when two people meet and a *transactional response* to this stimulus. In order to analyse the transactions, i.e. what is exchanged between people, in a targeted way, it is necessary to take a closer look at the people involved. Berne (1966) states, in this regard, that when observing people's spontaneous social activity, "from time to time people show noticeable changes in posture, viewpoint, voice, vocabulary, and other aspects of behavior" (p. 23). He explains these changes in behaviour as changes in the emotional realm. The changes are so profound that Berne speaks of the change in the person's "**ego state**" at these moments (Berne, 1966, p. 23).

> **Definition**
> According to Berne (1966), an **ego state** can "be described phenomenologically as a coherent system of feelings and operationally as a set of coherent behavior patterns" (p. 23).

Before we get to the actual transactions, we will examine the various ego states of humans in a little more detail below.

2.4.1 The Ego States: A Model of the Structure of the Human Personality

When we approach the ego states, it is important to understand that a human being is always to be considered psychically as a unity and cannot be divided into different psychic components. In an adult human being, all ego states are always present, but at any given time only one ego state is occupied or active with energy (Berne, 1966).

The ego states (see ◘ Fig. 2.3) can be described according to Berne (1966) as follows:
1. The **childhood ego** comes from our childhood and enables us to be in our thinking, feeling and behaviour as we were then as a child. The "child in us" is still present - regardless of our age - so that we can still use its potentials. In the childhood self, we are very close to our feelings. We laugh or cry when we feel like it, we are spontaneous and creative, and we do and take things according to what we feel like at the moment. We can be kind and friendly, but also excited and rebellious.

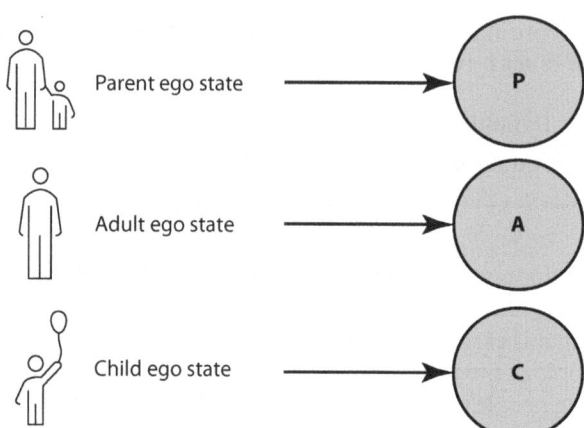

Fig. 2.3 Structural model with three ego states according to Eric Berne. The structural model of the three ego states according to Berne is a central model of transactional analysis. It consists of three ego states: The childhood ego, the parent ego and the adult ego. These three ego states are present in every adult human being. One ego state is active at any given time. (Source: Own representation based on Berne, 1984, p. 28)

2. We have experienced the **parent ego** with our parents, but also with other authority figures. In this ego state, our thinking, feeling and behaviour are oriented to our experience at that time. Back then, we were given boundaries, norms, permissions and prohibitions, rules and instructions, and so on. We have also experienced attention, help and care in this context. We have stored these impressions in us and pass them on to our environment today. In the course of time, we have internalised many of these impressions so profoundly that we still show corresponding behaviour towards other people today without reflecting on it.
3. The **adult ego** first forms in early childhood. When this ego state is activated or, in other words, energised, we are in the here and now. We are objective and logical, orient ourselves to objective realities, absorb factual context, weigh up options and, after weighing up the options, make decisions that make most sense from our point of view.

The individuality of the single person arises from how and in which contexts the different ego states are activated. Depending on the personal experiences made in the development of the different ego states, the person shows different behaviours in the ego states. In order to be able to carry out more precise analyses of communication processes, modern transactional analysis subdivides the childhood ego and the parent ego even further in the **functional model of the ego states** (Gührs & Nowak, 2014) (see ◘ Fig. 2.4).

Following Gührs and Nowak (2014), the ego states in the functional model are characterised as follows.

- **Childhood Ego**

The childhood ego is divided into the free childhood ego, the rebellious childhood ego, and the conformist childhood ego.
1. In the **free childhood ego**, we are directly in touch with ourselves and our feelings and needs. We are spontaneous, creative, we know what we feel like doing and we just act accordingly. We are playful and smart, but we can also be selfish and reckless. We focus only on ourselves in that moment.

2.4 · Transactional Analysis: The Answer to the Question of Why?

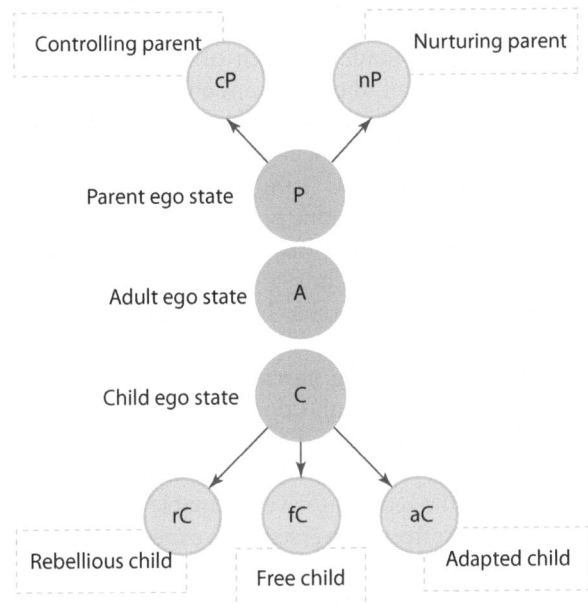

Fig. 2.4 Functional model of ego states. The functional model of ego states can be used to analyse communication processes in more detail. It is often used in transactional analysis to describe and understand inner and outer behaviour in more detail. (Source: Own representation based on Gührs and Nowak, 2014, p. 78)

2. The **adapted childhood ego** and the rebellious childhood ego respond to instructions, rules, and norms from our parents and other authorities, respectively. The reactions are opposite in the two ego states. People in the conformist childhood ego state look at what others expect of them and try to meet those expectations - even if they themselves want something different. They are usually reserved and put their needs behind those of others. Their view of the world and life is often one of their inadequacy, which manifests in anxiety, passivity, or even offended withdrawal. The adapted childhood ego does have its right to exist since human coexistence is hardly possible without being responsive to other people and a certain degree of adaptation.
3. When the **rebellious childhood ego** appears in a person, it usually reacts to the parent ego of another person as the adapted childhood ego does, but in such a way that it rejects the expectations. The rebellious childhood ego opposes these expectations vehemently and forcefully. And it also has a right to exist. After all, its powerful opposition is often followed by innovations that would not have been achieved on the old, predetermined paths.

- **Parent Ego**

In the functional model, the parent ego is divided into the critical-normative parent ego and the nurturing-caring parent ego.

1. The **critical-normative parent ego** behaves in an authoritarian manner. It establishes rules, sets limits and norms. At the same time, it also ensures that the norms and rules are adhered to. Destructive behaviour will be prevented by it. The critical-normative parent ego looks for faults and criticises other people. In order to exert control, it intimidates and thereby also creates a distance between

itself and others. The critical-normative parent ego and the rebellious childhood ego are made for each other. While the critical-normative parent ego strives to prevail, the rebellious childhood ego opposes and resists. In this way, a destructive and escalating, but very stable interaction can arise between people. The course of sometimes heated discussions between parents ("You will clean your room now!") and children ("It's tidy enough and besides, I don't feel like it!"), which everyone probably still remembers, is an example of this. If the perceived threat from the critical-normative parent ego becomes too great in the other person, withdrawal and compliance may occur. In this case, the conformist childhood ego has been activated, backing down and allowing someone else to exercise power over it.

2. The **nurturing-caring parent ego** takes care of others. It comforts, is loving, helps and supports, and does everything else to make others feel good. It also praises, encourages, and offers protection. These behaviours are very valuable in situations where they are truly and honestly needed. However, if they are imposed (the recipient is very capable of handling the situation at hand themselves), the effect is reversed. The expectation is that the adjusted childhood ego will respond and allow itself to be infantilised and deprived of its autonomy. In this case, the nurturing-caring parent ego shows its negative side.

Let us take a look at the different ego states in action:

▶ Case Study

Susan has been working at Construction Machines Smith Ltd for 4 years. She has an important interview this afternoon that will decide her future career. It is about a vacant position as project manager, which she would like to have. The project in question is very important for the company. Therefore, she will talk to the managing director John Smith personally. Susan activates her six ego states one after the other in the morning and thinks about the important conversation:

1. "Finally, it's time. Great, it's coming along. I heard the boss is a great guy. I must tell him about my last project. We all had fun! It was really something! I'm sorry it's over. I hope the new project is as great. I'll just ask him what he thinks about it." (free childhood ego)
2. "I'm sure I won't be able to eat anything today for lunch. I'm all tensed up. I don't know what to say. Maybe talk about the last project? Does the boss even care? I hope I don't forget anything. Why did I even apply for the job? I wonder what he wants to know. I'm sure I won't get a word out." (adapted childhood ego)
3. "I'll give him a piece of my mind. I'm not putting up with any more of this. Projects are all well and good, but always filling out those endless lists. Projects work without paperwork. The boss doesn't even know what we're doing. If he doesn't like the way I see things, I won't take the new job. I don't have to. He's got it coming!" (rebellious childhood ego)
4. "I know exactly how the land lies. I'll explain it to the manager in detail. Hard work leads to the goal. No pain, no gain. That applies to all situations in life. In project work, too. Let us see if he understands. I'll find simple words to teach him. The job is as good as mine." (critical-normative parent ego)

2.4 · Transactional Analysis: The Answer to the Question of Why?

5. "I already know exactly how to help him. He often looks overworked. I'm sure he's worried about all the projects. I will make him feel that with me working on the projects, everything will be fine. I've been around for so long and everyone always feels comfortable with me. Such harmonious togetherness is nice for everyone, isn't it?" (nurturing-caring parent ego)
6. "The job description says 'at least three completed projects and experience in project management as well as at least one project as a sub-project manager'. That's what I can offer: Four completed projects, one of which as a sub-project manager, as well as various training in project management. I fully meet the formal expectations. So it will be about the interpersonal. If he asks, I will present some of my successes. The way I've met the boss so far, I shouldn't lay it on too thick, he doesn't like that. Otherwise, I'll let him talk first and listen carefully. I should ask one or two interposed questions. Taking all of this into account, I think I might have quite a good chance of getting the job." (adult ego) ◄

> **Important**
> With the help of the book "The Constructive Conversation" ("Das konstruktive Gespräch") by Manfred Gührs and Claus Nowak (2014), you can deepen the topic of transactional analysis very clearly. The ego states with associated behaviours are described in tabular form on pages 81 and 82. However, to our knowledge, the book is currently only available in German.

> **Reflection task: Conscious interactions from the different ego states**
> In our experience, it is fun to consciously play with the ego states. Please find a familiar person and act out the different ego states using examples from your everyday life. Everyday situations could be, for example, conversations with a superior person at work, with your parents or also with people towards whom you might feel insecure. In each case, please ask yourself how the change in ego state affects your communication with the person in question.

2.4.2 Transactions: What Happens Between People

In the model of transactional analysis, people are in exactly one ego state at any given time. Their behaviour as well as their thinking and feeling are determined by this ego state. Transactions, therefore, take place between the ego states of the people involved. Therefore, a critical-normative parent ego meets a rebellious childhood ego or an adult ego meets an adapted childhood ego, and so on. Each personality is different, each ego state differently expressed; the possibilities are endless. Nevertheless, there are patterns in interaction that can be observed again and again (Berne, 1966).

The *complementary* or *parallel transaction* (both terms are used in the literature) could be captioned "The expected happens." The person who sends out the transactional stimulus has a certain idea of how and in what ego state his counterpart should react. If this idea is met, the **transaction** is **complementary** (Berne, 1966) (see ◘ Fig. 2.5).

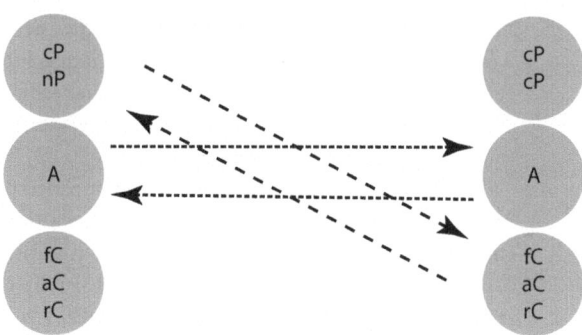

Fig. 2.5 Complementary or parallel transactions. In the figure, the critical-normative parent ego expects a response from the childhood ego (dotted arrows), see case study Frank Wilson - trainee. The adult ego expects a response from the other adult ego (dotted arrows, see case study John and Anna Smith). (Source: Own representation based on Berne, 1984, p. 33)

► Case Study

Frank Wilson says with a serious face to a trainee whose workplace is very untidy: "Clean up this mess immediately!" His ego state is the critical-normative parent ego. Frank Wilson unconsciously expects the trainee to respond in the childhood ego. And that is exactly what happens. He crosses his arms and replies angrily, "I don't feel like it. I just cleaned up yesterday. I guess it's my business what the place looks like." Frank Wilson replies louder, "I'm not putting up with you anymore! You're going to do what I tell you!"

Everything that happens is not surprising. Complementary transactions are very stable forms of interaction. Basically, the script of the dialogue is already set. Frank Wilson continues to threaten, the trainee counters. Both get angrier and angrier and the situation escalates further. At some point, the dialogue is interrupted and action is taken. In this constellation (see ◘ Fig. 2.6), the whole thing could escalate to the point where the HR department has to be called in. ◄

Of course, another complementary transaction is also possible:

The trainee might activate the adapted childhood self, flinch, blush, and say, "Excuse me, I forgot to clean up. I'll start right away." In this case, too, something happens that fits the opening sentence, "Clean up this mess right now!"

Frank Wilson (cP):	"Clean up this mess right now!"
Trainee (rC):	"I don't feel like it. I just cleaned up yesterday. I guess it's my business what the place looks like."

or

Trainee (aC):	"Excuse me, I forgot to clean up. I'll start right away."

2.4 · Transactional Analysis: The Answer to the Question of Why?

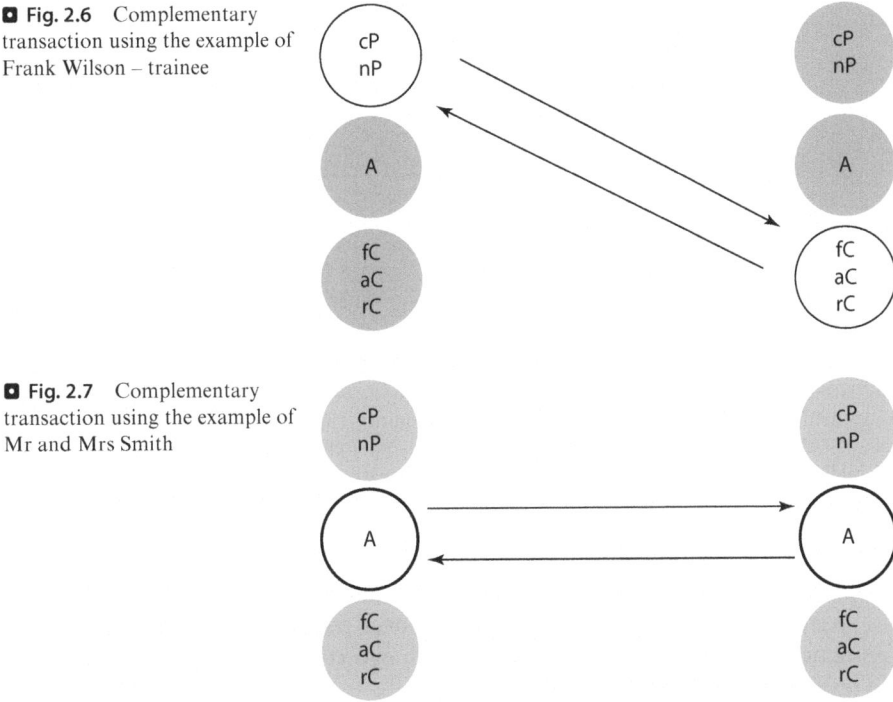

Fig. 2.6 Complementary transaction using the example of Frank Wilson – trainee

Fig. 2.7 Complementary transaction using the example of Mr and Mrs Smith

Transactions can occur in any combination of ego states. The important thing is that the transactional stimulus is responded to as expected (Berne, 1966). In our experience, the adult ego state has often proven successful in professional contexts. In this, it is possible to work on common solutions in a fact-oriented way. Let us look at the following example dialogue between John Smith and his wife Anna (see ◘ Fig. 2.7).

► **Case Study**

John Smith (A):	"Where can I find the Thompson file?"
Anna Smith (A):	"In the middle filing cabinet in the first folder."

◄

A sober and factual question is answered just as soberly and factually. There are also complementary transactions between two critical-normative parent egos. For example, at a parents' evening, two fathers in the critical-normative parent ego might talk at length about the youth of today and their lack of a sense of order.

? Reflection task: Personal experiences with complementary transactions
What are examples of complementary transactions that you remember from personal conversations? Which ego states were activated in the respective situation?

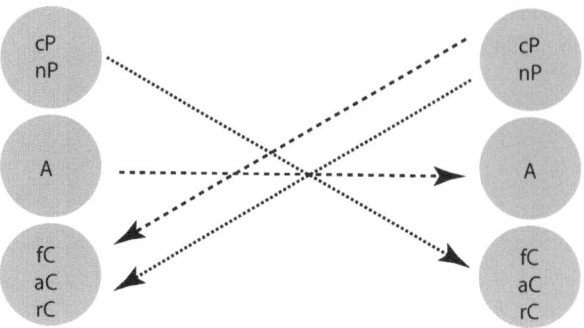

□ **Fig. 2.8** Crossed transactions. As a rule, the adult ego also expects a reaction from the other adult ego (dashed arrows). If the critical-normative parent ego of the other person responds instead, this has an irritating effect (see case study John and Anna Smith). The same applies, for example (dotted arrow), if the critical-normative parent ego ("That was a poor effort. You can do better.") addresses the childhood ego of the other person and the critical-normative parent ego answers instead ("It's not your job to evaluate my work. You better watch what you say."). (Source: Own representation based on Berne, 1984, p. 34)

When the expected does not happen, but something else does, transactional analysis speaks of a **crossed transaction** or crossover transaction (Berne, 1966). The transactional stimulus is directed at a certain ego state, but surprisingly another one responds (see e.g. □ Fig. 2.8).

► Case Study

John Smith asks his wife Anna in a matter-of-fact tone of voice, "Where can I find the Thompson file?" She replies seriously: "You'd better keep in mind where you put your files."

As a rule, a question in the adult ego also expects an answer in the adult ego and not - as in this case - in the critical-normative parent ego, which is addressed to the childhood ego. John Smith will probably be surprised or irritated. In this case, his wife is not responding to the actual question about the file, but something in the past. Perhaps over time, the situations in which he asked her for something he could have known or done himself added up and reached a limit now. There could be many reasons. Nevertheless, John Smith will be irritated by the crossed transaction and the intended result of his transaction – the information on the whereabouts of the Thompson file- does not happen at the moment.

How could John Smith deal with the situation? He could respond with a parallel transaction, e.g. in the rebellious childhood ego: "I don't need you to tell me whether or not I can remember where I put my files." In this case, communication is likely to stabilise. His wife will likely remain in the critical-normative parent ego. It is now no longer about the file, but about who behaves towards whom in the past, today and in the future. John Smith does not come one step closer to the file.

It would be more favourable if he would also schedule a crossed transaction. The objective, in this case, would be to get his wife to activate her adult ego as well. He could continue to energise his adult ego and answer: "Do you have the impression that I bother you with trivial matters? We can talk about it right away, but the client is waiting for an answer. So could you please help me first and tell me where the Thompson file is?" In this way, it is often possible to persuade another person to leave an unproductive and non-goal-oriented ego state and switch to a productive ego state. ◄

> **Important**
> Every ego state has its justification. A person is only complete in his personality if he has all ego states at his disposal. In professional contexts, Gührs and Nowak agree that three ego states are to be preferred because they support people in dealing with each other productively. The adult ego is the objective, evaluating part of the personality. It asks the question of the meaning of a decision. The free childhood self is the creative and innovative part. It asks the question of what a person feels like doing. The nurturing parent ego gives support and helps others. It asks what is good for oneself and others. When preparing a decision, it is worthwhile to question the three productive ego states and to weigh their answers up again in the adult ego state. (Gührs & Nowak, 2014).

The third type of transaction is the **covert transaction**. The covert transaction runs as a second transaction next to the superficially recognisable transaction. It is expressed through the behaviour of the sender who, for example, says something but shows incongruent behaviour. In transactional analysis, the overt level is referred to as the social level and the covert level as the psychological level (Berne, 1966; Gührs & Nowak, 2014).

> ► Case Study
> In response to a question from Ms. Miller, Mr. Smith's secretary, in the nurturing parent ego ("How are you?"), the trainee answers on a social level from the adult ego ("I'm fine."). In contrast, the trainee's tone of voice and facial expression reveal the exact opposite message from the free child ego ("I feel lousy as hell."). The covert transaction can be perceived with varying degrees of clarity. On the emotional level, Ms. Miller may perceive the message as an uneasy or queasy feeling. ◄

Another example of covert transactions is irony. The person addressed in an ironic way is in a dilemma. Two messages arrive, one overt and one covert. But what should the recipient react to? If they react to the psychological level of the message, the other person could deny it - something else was said. Ignoring it would be a second possibility. In that case, you might be left with an uneasy feeling. Or cross the transaction? From the adult ego, the question could be asked, "What do you mean?"

In any case, covert transactions, such as irony make purposeful and productive communication much more difficult. Covert transactions are often responsible for all sorts of confusions, tangles and misunderstandings in human communication. They are also frequently used with manipulative intent.

For example, a grandmother might sigh and say to her grandson, "I'm doing fine on my own. I know you have so much to do."

> **Important**
> In professional contexts, we believe that covert transactions should be avoided. They not only make targeted communication more difficult but can also have a lasting negative impact on the professional relationship. Irony in particular, if misunderstood, can lead to deep grievances and conflicts that are difficult to mediate.

2.4.3 People's Views of Life

The last element of transactional analysis that we would like to look at in order to understand human communication is people's different **views of life**, which can be characterised as people's basic attitudes towards their own lives and towards relationships with others. Thomas A. Harris (1969), a close collaborator of Eric Berne, differentiates in his book "I'm OK – You're OK" between four possible views of life or possibilities of self-perception and perception of others, which are illustrated in the following scheme (Harris, 1969, pp. 37–53.) (see ◘ Fig. 2.9).

The foundations for how a person sees themselves and others are laid in childhood. The way parents treat their child determines the child's self-image and later that of the adult. The child asks themselves: Who and how am I? The answers the child receives to their questions manifest themselves in the child's self-image. If they receive the message, "You are all right and you are valuable just as you are," they will adopt this image, just as they will internalise contrary images as well. A similar thing happens with their view of other people. If the child perceives their environment as friendly and valuable, they will internalise it just as they would an environment that they meet with distrust. The view of life is the result of this process, although it does not have to be constant throughout, but can vary depending on the context (Gührs & Nowak, 2014; Harris, 1969).

Everyone involved in the communication process has such a view of life in the here and now. Depending on the form it takes, communication is coloured differently. In the following, let us take a closer look at the four views of life based on Harris (Gührs & Nowak, 2014; Harris, 1969):

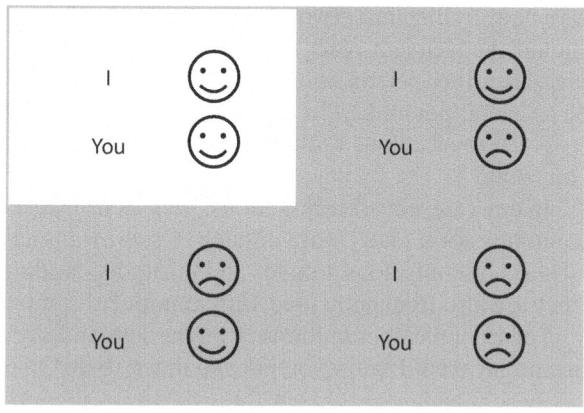

◘ Fig. 2.9 The four basic views of life in transactional analysis. Of the four basic ways of seeing oneself and others, the life view "I'm OK, You're OK" is a favourable condition for the success of human communication. (Source: Own representation based on Harris, 1969, pp. 37–53)

2.4 · Transactional Analysis: The Answer to the Question of Why?

1. **I am okay, you are okay.**
   This view of life forms the most favourable prerequisite for human communication to succeed. People perceive themselves and others as good and valuable. Communication is open, trusting and appreciative. It does not necessarily have to be free of contradiction and differing opinions. However, with such an attitude it is possible to keep conflicts to the factual level and to find compromises regardless of the person.
2. **I am okay, you are not okay.**
   People with this outlook on life are convinced of themselves and feel superior to others. They are impatient with others and take over tasks. They're always there to get credit for success but in case of failure they put the blame on others. They appear arrogant in communication and behave deprecatingly towards other people.
3. **I am not okay, you are okay.**
   Life feels difficult and overwhelming for people with this view of life. They feel inferior to other people and devalue themselves as a person. According to this view of life, other people can do everything better and have fewer faults and flaws than they do. This view of life is very stressful for the person so that the person temporarily seeks relief in the view of life described below, "I am not okay, you are not okay". The failure of others is thereby deliberately brought about in order to show oneself, "I may be inadequate, but the others are no better."
4. **I am not okay, you are not okay.**
   Such a view of life is associated with a sense of great futility. Myself and also others are not valuable. Everything and everyone in the life of such a person is negative. If something positive happens that does not fit into this view of life, it is devalued and denied. Such people are not very open to constructive suggestions for solutions, because they have the urge to have their internalised view of life confirmed.

> **Important**
> In our experience, human beings have a preferred view of life but can change to any other view of life depending on the situation. Therefore, a spontaneous change can occur in challenging and stressful situations. A person's preferred life view or basic attitude is deeply rooted in their psyche. It is real and true for them. Therefore, a person will defend their basic attitude even when objective facts contradict it.

► **Example: Relief Through Devaluation**
A person who does not feel okay and receives praise and recognition for their work feels mentally and sometimes even physically unwell. To relieve themselves, this person will often try to devalue their performance. For example, John Smith, who wants to praise an employee with the sentence, "Great job, keep it up," might receive the following response: "Oh, that was just luck. Every dog has is day." ◄

? Reflection task: My personal view of life

What is your preferred outlook on life? Think of situations that were challenging or even stressful for you, a job interview, for example. How did you feel and what did you think about your interviewer? Experience shows that one's attitude towards oneself and others can be different in concrete situations. Please think consciously about encounters with other people in which you felt really good and which gave you pleasure. What were your attitude and that of your counterpart in the situation? Were there situations where it was completely different and you felt extremely uncomfortable talking to another person? What attitudes did you both have in the situation?

2.5 Communication According to Schulz von Thun

When people meet each other, they also communicate. Messages are exchanged in verbal or non-verbal form (behaviour). We have since learned that the meaning of a message for the receiver depends on the content, the relationship to the sender, the sender and receiver themselves, and the context. At the beginning of the 1980s, Friedemann Schulz von Thun presented his concept of the four sides of a message, which is still popular today. According to his statement, he tried to bring the basic approaches to communication research under one roof (Schulz von Thun, 2013, p. 14).

2.5.1 The Four Sides of a Message

According to Schulz von Thun, a message has four sides or aspects . It has factual content, a relationship component, a self-revelation component, and an appeal component (Schulz von Thun, 2013). This relationship is illustrated in ◘ Fig. 2.10.

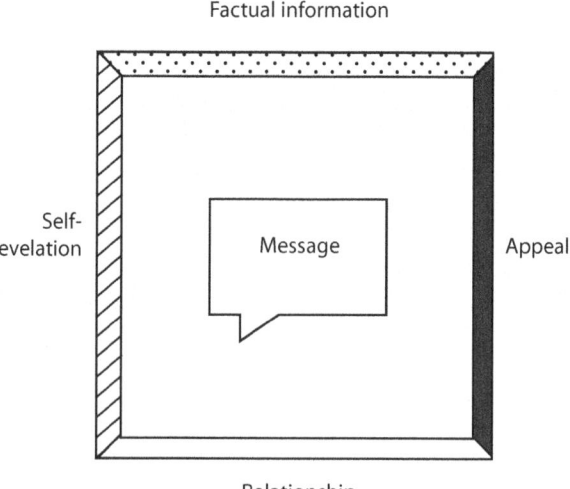

◘ Fig. 2.10 The four sides of a message. Schulz von Thun's four-sided model is also known as the communication square and states that every message always has several levels: Subject level, relationship level, self-revelation level, appeal level. This model can be used to describe communication that is disturbed by misunderstandings, for example. (Source: Own representation based on Schulz von Thun, 2013, p. 15)

2.5 · Communication According to Schulz von Thun

In the following, we will give you an overview of the concept formulated by Schulz von Thun. The different parts can be characterised as follows:

1. **Factual content**: The factual content is encoded in some form by the sender of the message and has to be decoded again by the receiver. Such encodings can be language, symbols or other forms of signs (e.g. sign language for the deaf). In order to be able to transmit and receive the factual content reliably, the sender and receiver necessarily must have the same "default settings" so to speak. If the sender and receiver only speak and understand different languages, a transmitted message cannot be decoded or translated by the receiver. If the "settings" of the sender and receiver do not match, misunderstandings will occur. These can go so far that the recipient does not understand the content at all. Often it only takes single words that were interpreted differently or not understood at all. Therefore, it would easily be possible to make this text at least difficult to understand, if not unreadable, through the extensive use of foreign words, nested sentences, undefined abbreviations, etc. In this context, Schulz von Thun refers to the **Hamburg intelligibility model** (Langer, Schulz von Thun, & Tausch, 1974, 1981). This was developed by Friedemann Reinhard Tausch, Schulz von Thun and Inghard Langer in the early 1970s. According to this model, intelligibility is based on four pillars (cf. Schulz von Thun, 2013):
   - simplicity in linguistic formulation,
   - structure of the text,
   - brevity and conciseness, and
   - additional stimuli or stimulating stylistic device.

2. **Relationship**: At its core is the question of how sender and receiver define their relationship. Words are chosen and behaviour is adapted accordingly. If two friends meet and one greets the other with the sentence "Well, my friend, how are you?", this sentence is probably congruent with the friendly relationship of the two. Now, we keep the sentence "Well, my friend, how are you?" and only change the relationship. What meaning does this sentence take on when you use it with a complete stranger? It would certainly be interesting to see how your manager would take the phrase. Watzlawick et al. also pointed out the relational aspect of all human communication in their second axiom on human communication - as we learned in ▶ Sect. 2.3. If the relationship definition of the sender and receiver match, there is a high probability that the message of the message will be understood as it is meant. If the receiver of the message has a different relationship definition, irritations and misunderstandings will occur.

3. **Self-revelation** or *self-disclosure*: When a person communicates, they always reveal something about themselves. The language or the way someone expresses themselves reveals something about their linguistic environment. A person's behaviour gives us clues as to how they are feeling at the moment. Is the person excited or calm, tense or relaxed, embarrassed or confident …? Behaviour reveals our own internalised attitude with which we approach another person (for example, with appreciation or devaluation). Even when a person tries to suppress or cover up their attitude or emotions, something comes across to us. Sometimes it is just a slight feeling of irritation.

4. **Appeal**: Although some dialogues on TV do not support the idea that people usually communicate purposefully, there is usually an intention behind a message. Schulz von Thun writes about this, hardly anything is said unintentionally (Schulz von Thun, 2013, p. 32). The intention behind a message can be stated openly or kept hidden. In the second case, the sender is trying to manipulate the receiver. In the case of a manipulative intent, the other three sides are usually deliberately aligned accordingly to further enhance the effect of covert influence.

> **Important**
> To deepen your understanding of Schulz von Thun's model, we recommend his very readable book "Talking to each other 1: Disruptions and clarifications" ("Miteinander reden 1: Störungen und Klärungen") (2013), which has been reprinted many times and is also available in paperback. However, to our knowledge, the book is currently only available in German.

2.5.2 Congruent and Incongruent Communication

According to Schulz von Thun's model, messages have four sides. Every message transmitted in verbal form includes them. In purely non-verbal messages, the factual content usually remains empty, unless the sender and receiver communicate in a sign language. Each message has multiple sides with information content. These sides may be explicitly formulated or implicitly inferred (e.g., via the sender's behaviour). The implicit part of a message is often transmitted non-verbally. They are, so to speak, "between the lines" (Schulz von Thun, 2013). Depending on the relationship between implicit and explicit messages, the message can be **congruent** or **incongruent**:

> **Definition**
>
> **Congruent message**: A message is called congruent if all the signals point in the same direction if they are coherent in themselves (Schulz von Thun, 2013, p. 39). Example: If Frank Wilson yells at a trainee in a rage, with his face flushed and his eyes wide open with the words "I'm not willing to be taken for a ride by you any longer!", then what is said and the behaviour are certainly congruent.

> **Definition**
>
> **Incongruent messages** are messages in which the linguistic and non-linguistic signals do not match (Schulz von Thun, 2013, p. 39).
> Example: If some colleagues of Construction Machines Smith Ltd meet in the evening for bowling and a member of their team says with a poker face "Nice shot!" after a fellow player has only hit the gutter for the second time in a row, the incongruity of the statement and the actual message is relatively easy to understand for the person addressed.

Incongruent messages are not consistent in themselves. In these cases, what is said is more or less clearly incongruent with the other, non-linguistic signals. The receiver has various interpretation aids at their disposal to determine the actual message (Schulz von Thun, 2013). According to Schulz von Thun, Haley (1978) speaks in this context of the *qualification of a message*. Therefore, the context, the way of phrasing, the facial expressions and gestures as well as the tone of voice can provide clues for the qualification of a message (Schulz von Thun, 2013).

The situation becomes more complex when messages are transported via the relationship level. On the relationship level, it is important that the sender and receiver define the relationship in the same way, otherwise, messages will be distorted and so misunderstood or incomprehensible (Schulz von Thun, 2013; Watzlawick et al., 1968).

► Case Study

In a clarified relationship based on mutual appreciation, such as John and Anna Smith's, a sentence like the following may be uttered - with a friendly smile on the lips: "I have gone through this several times. On second thought, your decision was pretty idiotic." Although the sentence is incongruent with her facial expression, there is a good chance that intended implicit messages, presumably something like "I'm with you. Feel free to talk to me first next time. I'll be happy to help you." will get through. However, there is no guarantee for this even in such a clarified relationship.

Now let us imagine that the sentence is spoken between colleagues whose relationship is not clear. A smile is ambiguous, as it can express affection or contempt. The recipient now has a choice: If they consider the message congruent and feel offended, this person is not only called an idiot but also treated with contempt at the same time. Or do they view the banter as a warm up showing them compassion and help? The first message is far more likely to be understood than the second. Depending on the degree of incongruity, the receiver is increasingly irritated or even confused: How and to what should they respond? To what is said or to what they perceive in a different way? ◄

Especially in unresolved relationships, conflicts have to be expected in such cases. Another example of incongruence with potentially devastating effects is, in our experience, the use of irony in unresolved relationships. Even unintentionally, people can be deeply hurt by irony.

? Reflection task: Targeted use of incongruence in comedies
In comedies, the stylistic device of misunderstanding is often used. Next time you go to the cinema or watch television, pay attention to the incongruity of the actors' communication.

2.5.3 Communication: It's a Give and Take

Our previous considerations focused primarily on the sender of a message. The sender says something or behaves with the intention of communicating something to the receiver. They send their messages - with its multiple sides or facets - without knowing which message actually reaches the receiver and how. The receiver has to decode the message with the means at their disposal. Schulz von Thun uses the image of four ears to illustrate how the receiver of the message hears it. They hear with the factual ear, the relationship ear, the self-revelation ear and the appeal ear. Each ear receives its side of the message and decodes it. The result of the decoding depends on the receiver. The receiver processes the message, translates the different sides and reacts to them.

The translation and the reaction are completely subjective (see also ▶ Sect. 2.6; Schulz von Thun, 2013). In other words, anything can happen.

> ▶ Case Study
>
> The reaction to a kindly meant "Good morning, Mr. Wilson." by Karen Baker may well be: "Whether the morning is a good one, time will tell." Mr. Wilson responds, but to something other than the kindly meant "Good morning." He may have an unpleasant conversation coming up, or he may be waiting for an unpleasant incoming message. There are many potential reasons for this. Nevertheless, Karen Baker is confronted with the answer which, from her point of view, does not match her greeting at all. Perhaps she infers that Mr. Wilson does not mean her at all, but something unpleasantly different. Or perhaps she feels attacked. In that case, she may respond with, "I suppose saying good morning to each other is still ok, isn't it?" And so on. ◀

The example shows that it makes no sense to consider the two interlocutors individually. Human communication always involves at least two, whose actions and reactions influence each other. The sender sends their message in their way, the receiver receives the message in their way and reacts to it in their way, so closing the circle (Schulz von Thun, 2013; Watzlawick et al., 1968).

As mentioned, human communication is circular - without beginning and end. The question of who acts first and who reacts when two people meet makes no sense. Whoever says something first might already be responding to a perceived behaviour of the other. Or linking to something in their shared past. Again, it is a matter of individual punctuation where the subjective starting point of communication is set. The receiver will also set one. Where it is up to him (Schulz von Thun, 2013; Watzlawick et al., 1968).

Schulz von Thun (2013) goes even further by speaking of a *supersummative equation* (p. 97) in communication. The interaction of two people who influence each other and thereby develop a momentum of their own so brings about more than the sum of the two parts. What happens in communication can be explained in retrospect and with appropriate analysis, but it cannot be predicted.

> ❓ **Reflection task: The principle of emergence**
> Have you ever consciously experienced in cooperation with other people that the course of the communication evolved and surpassed your expectations? Please recall this conversation and try to understand what happened in the mutual exchange. Please also research the principle of emergence.

2.6 Constructivist Perspective on Communication

In our view, a radical way of looking at communication is to see it as fully constructivist, that is, to adopt a **constructivist view**. Keller, Knoblauch and Reichertz (2013) state that constructivism generally assumes that reality is not a mere 'positive' given, but a construction, though by no means an arbitrary one (p. 9).

> **Definition**
>
> A **constructivist view** in the context of communication means that people first process what reaches them in terms of sensory impressions and then create their subjective reality from this.

Watzlawick et al. and Schulz von Thun are also representatives of a constructivist view of communication. For example, Schulz von Thun (2013) chooses the following heading for a chapter: The incoming message: A 'work of art' by the receiver (p. 67). Ultimately, such a view means that while the sender may send statements with intended messages, it depends on the receiver what they understand. So the receiver does not react to what is said, nor to what is heard, but to what is understood (Schulz von Thun, 2013; Watzlawick et al., 1968).

Such a strictly constructivist model of communication has its justification. In our view, however, it often reaches its limits in the application, since the human being is usually a black box when observing communication processes. In the introspection of one's communication, it makes perfect sense to reflect on oneself and the way messages are dealt with.

> **Summary in Key Terms**
> - In this chapter, we have dealt with the content of **metacommunication**, i.e. communication about communication based on systems and concepts.
> - Fundamentals:
>   - Human communication can be simplified as a verbal or non-verbal exchange of **messages** between a **sender** and at least one **receiver** (*sender-receiver model* according to Shannon and Weaver, 1972).
>   - People always exchange **factual content** and messages on the relationship level at the same time, while also revealing something about themselves and pursuing an intention with their communication.
> - Human communication can be analysed by means of various **models and approaches** (individually and in combination). We have dealt with three very well-known approaches in this chapter: The *five axioms* according to Watzlawick et al. (1968), the *four-sided square* according to Schulz von Thun (2013) and *transactional analysis* according to Eric Berne (1966).
>   - *Five axioms* of Watzlawick, Beavin and Jackson (1968) on human communication:

1. You cannot not communicate.
2. Every communication has a content and a relationship aspect such that the latter classifies the former.
3. The nature of a relationship is contingent upon the punctuation of the communicational sequences between the communicants.
4. Human beings communicate both digitally and analogically.
5. All communicational interchanges are either symmetrical or complementary, depending on whether they are based on equality or difference.

- *Four-sides model* of a message according to Schulz von Thun (2013):
    - Subject level
    - Relationship level
    - Self-revelation level
    - Appeal level
- *Transactional analysis* according to Berne (1984): Communication takes place on the basis of the ego states active in transactions (parent ego, adult ego, childhood ego). Symmetrical or complementary transactions, which are expected as such by all communicating parties, are evidence of successful communication, whereas crossed or hidden transactions can prove problematic.
- The communicators' **views of life**, as formulated by Harris (1969), for example, or the perceived **congruence** of the messages transmitted also have an impact on the success of communication.
- **Constructivist view** of communication: The received message always depends to a large extent on the receiver themselves.

Literature

Berne, E. (1961). *Transactional analysis in psychotherapy*. Grove Press.
Berne, E. (1966). *Games people play. The psychology of human relationships*. Deutsch.
Berne, E. (1984). Spiele der Erwachsenen [Adult Games]. Reinbek: Rowohlt.
Cambridge University Press. (n.d.-a). Axiom. In *Cambridge advanced learner's dictionary & thesaurus*. Retrieved July 21, 2021, from https://dictionary.cambridge.org/dictionary/english/axiom
Cambridge University Press. (n.d.-b). Communication. In *Cambridge academic content dictionary*. Retrieved July 21, 2021, from https://dictionary.cambridge.org/dictionary/english/communication
Gührs, M., & Nowak, C. (2014). *Das konstruktive Gespräch. Ein Leitfaden für Beratung, Unterricht und Mitarbeiterführung mit Konzepten der Transaktionsanalyse* [The constructive conversation. A guide to coaching, teaching and personnel management involving concepts from transaction analysis] (7th ed.). Christa Limmer.
Haley, J. (1978). *Gemeinsamer Nenner Interaktion [Common denominator interaction]*. Pfeiffer.
Harris, T. A. (1969). I'm OK, you're OK. A practical guide to transactional analysis. Harper & Row.
Keller, R., Knoblauch, H., & Reichertz, J. (2013). *Kommunikativer Konstruktivismus* [Communicative constructivism]. Springer.
Langer, I., Schulz von Thun, F., & Tausch, R. (1974). *Verständlichkeit in Schule, Verwaltung, Politik und Wissenschaft* [Comprehensibility in school, administration, politics and science]. E. Reinhardt.
Langer, I., Schulz von Thun, F., & Tausch, R. (1981). *Sich verständlich ausdrücken* [Expressing oneself comprehensibly] (2nd ed.). E. Reinhardt.

Literature

Lubienetzki, U., & Schüler-Lubienetzki, H. (2016). *Was wir uns wie sagen und zeigen. Menschliche Kommunikation* [What we say and show to each other and how. Human communication] (study letter of the Fresenius University of Applied Sciences online plus GmbH). Hochschule Fresenius online plus GmbH.

Merriam-Webster. (n.d.). Syntax. In Merriam-Webster.com *dictionary*. Retrieved on July 25, 2021, from https://www.merriam-webster.com/dictionary/syntax

Oxford University Press. (n.d.). Semantics. In *Oxford advanced learner's dictionary*. Retrieved July 25, 2021, from https://www.oxfordlearnersdictionaries.com/definition/english/semantics

Schulz von Thun, F. (2013). *Miteinander Reden 1 – Störungen und Klärungen* [Talking to one another 1 – Disturbances and clarifications] (50th ed.). Rowohlt.

Shannon, C. E., & Weaver, W. (1972). *The mathematical theory of communication* (5th ed.). University of Illinois Press.

Watzlawick, P., Beavin, J. H., & Jackson, D. D. (1968). *Pragmatics of human communication. A study of interactional patterns, pathologies, and paradoxes*. London: Faber and Faber.

Communication Styles and Patterns

Basic Typologies and Patterns of Communication

Contents

3.1 Eight Communication Styles According to Schulz von Thun – 38

3.2 Tools and Instruments for the Study of Communication – 43
3.2.1 (Vicious) Circles in Communication – 44
3.2.2 Values and Development Square – 47
3.2.3 The Drama Triangle – 50

Literature – 55

The explanations in this chapter are based on the following study brief: Lubienetzki, U. and Schüler-Lubienetzki, H. (2016). WHAT WE SAY AND SHOW EACH OTHER AND HOW. HUMAN COMMUNICATION. Study letter of the Fresenius University of Applied Sciences (Hochschule Fresenius) online plus GmbH. Idstein: Hochschule Fresenius online plus GmbH.

© Springer-Verlag GmbH Germany, part of Springer Nature 2022
U. Lubienetzki, H. Schüler-Lubienetzki, *How We Talk to Each Other - The Messages We Send With Our Words and Body Language*, https://doi.org/10.1007/978-3-662-64437-9_3

Communication is not something abstract. Each an everyone of us experiences it every day. Moreover, we can observe it at any time and examine it for observable patterns. In this way, various basic typologies of human communication styles and specific communication patterns have already been identified. We can use different "tools" to study styles and patterns in communication.

After reading this chapter in-depth, you will be able to ...
- Differentiate and identify eight **communication styles** according to Schulz von Thun (2008).
- Recognise and explain **vicious circles** in communication.
- Explain the role of **values and principles** in communication and highlight the influence they can have on communication when exaggerated.
- Explain the origin and appearance of **drama triangles**.

3.1 Eight Communication Styles According to Schulz von Thun

The term *communication style* is closely linked to the work of Schulz von Thun. These are fundamental patterns that we observe again and again in human communication. Every person is individual and communicates individually. The identification of patterns allows us to highlight similarities in communication in order to analyse them systematically. From our point of view, trying to distinguish patterns according to a person's gender - to anticipate it here - bears the risk of depicting clichés and stereotypes. We, therefore, join Schulz von Thun (2008), who does not differentiate his eight communication styles according to gender. Therefore, he writes, while there are styles that are considered 'typically feminine' or 'typically masculine,' however, since 'everything is in everyone,' I did not want to contribute to the solidification of such stereotypes (p. 15).

Let us take a brief look at the eight communication styles identified by Schulz von Thun (see **Fig. 3.1**).

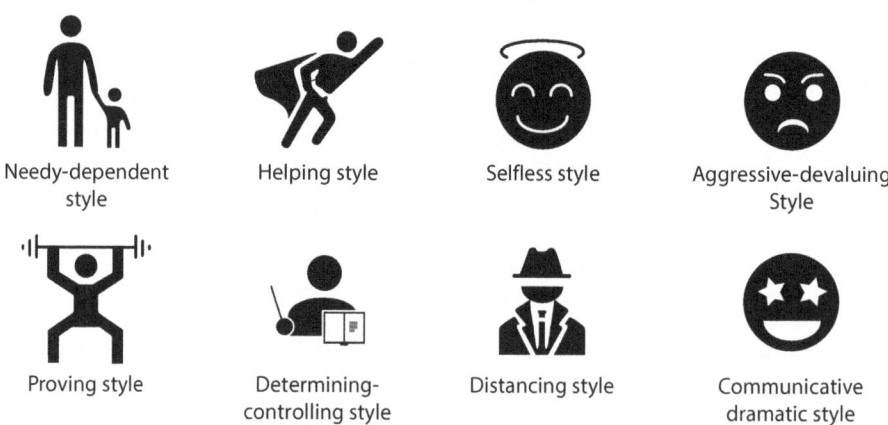

Fig. 3.1 Eight typical communication styles according to Schulz von Thun. (Source: Schulz von Thun, 2008)

3.1 · Eight Communication Styles According to Schulz von Thun

> **Important**
> Detailed descriptions of communication styles can be found in the book "Miteinander reden 2 - Stile, Werte und Persönlichkeitsentwicklung" (Schulz von Thun, 2008). However, to our knowledge, the book is currently only available in German.

- **Needy-Dependent Communication Style – "I Can't Do This, Please Help Me"**

Every human being starts out small. As an infant, they are completely dependent on their parents. Over time, the human being continues to develop, learns the many things of daily life, becomes more and more independent and is at some point able to ensure their survival. Even in the life of an adult, there are phases in which they want to be cared for and protected. Likewise, there are phases in which a person wants to act on their own, prove something to themselves, and be independent of other people. Toddlers, for example, can fly into a rage when they want to show themselves and others skills and initially fail. Humans are programmed to learn in order to get better and adapt to their environment. But if we are honest, it is certainly pleasant for many from time to time, even as adults, to be cared for as they once were as children.

People who use the needy-dependent communication style try to get others to care for them and help them. Some people use the style in selected cases because they have learned that people then take an unpleasant task off their hands, for example. If the need for help is deeper, the person has the basic attitude "I'm not okay" or there are possibly beliefs behind it, which could be: "I do everything wrong. I can't do anything on my own." So the needy-dependent style becomes the main communication style.

When we meet such a person, their sad look, their gestures seeking help, their occasional sighing and their quite clearly expressed pleas lead us to feel that this person needs to be saved. All of their statements convey the message, "I can't do this. Please help me." At the factual content level, requests and appeals are explicitly made. Self-revelation and appeal sides express unequivocally that help is urgently needed. Both verbally and nonverbally, the message of need for help is sent. The relationship side is particularly interesting, expressing, "I am small and weak and you are strong and competent." Such a relational offer can be very seductive to others. Who would not want to be strong and competent? If the other person takes this bait, the goal of the person seeking help is achieved. Especially people who want to experience themselves as rescuers or helpers are a perfect fit for the needy-dependent communication style. They just show complementary behaviour and are just waiting to be asked for help by others. Let us take a look at the next communication style.

- **Helping Communication Style – "I'll Do It (for You)"**

As said before: The helping communication style fits specially to the needy-dependent communication style described before. People who prefer to communicate in this style want to feel strong and independent. After all, the helping communication style expresses, "Don't worry, I can do this and I will. I don't need help." At the same time, this communication style also contains an element that expresses a certain superiority to others. The helper commits themselves to help others so to speak "from above" and not at the same level. This results in the special susceptibility to the needy-dependent style, since it makes the other person small so that they have to look up.

The helping communication style reveals a self that expresses strength and resilience. "I'll do it (for you)" or "I'll take care of it (for you)" can be such top-down helping messages. On the appeal side, recommendations are primarily sent; their own wishes do not seem to exist. Their own neediness is suppressed by the helper, e.g. because a deep fear of showing this to other people and appearing weak is anchored inside. The relationship side is also particularly interesting in this case since the basic message in this communication style is that others are helped because the helper feels superior. Towards a needy-dependent communicating person, this all works very well. However, it is different when the other person does not want any help or does not want to be saved. If both communicate in a helping style, i.e. symmetrically, the encounter can escalate into a mutual attempt to outdo each other in their respective superiority and independence.

- **Selfless Communication Style – "That Was Just a Fluke ..."**

People who communicate in the selfless style also have an urge to help others. However, a crucial difference from the helping communication style is that the person communicating in the selfless style make themselves small. Such a person feels unimportant and thinks they are worth nothing. By sacrificing themselves for others, such a person acquires a sense of their usefulness. The feeling of one's unimportance and worthlessness goes so far as to repel messages that mean the opposite. For them, praise and recognition of one's achievement are almost unbearable and must be promptly devalued. "That was nothing ...", "That was just coincidence/luck ..." or also "I know, otherwise I am/it is different." are such sentences with which the selfless person tries to set the personal world view straight again.

Accordingly, in the selfless style, a person sends as a self-revelation the message "I'm (worth) nothing." and appeals "Please tell me how you want me to be". At the relational level, others are signalled that only they matter, and their needs are the ones that count. People who want to feel superior readily accept such an offer of a relationship. However, the style can also trigger contempt in others when they feel the need to communicate on the same level and this is prevented by the selfless style and the view "I'm not ok, you're ok" by the communication partner. A person communicating in an aggressive-devaluing style may even be tempted to further degrade the self-degrading person.

- **Aggressive-Devaluing Communication Style – "Offense Is the Best Defence"**

People in the aggressive-devaluing style are condescending towards others and have the need to make other people small and to keep them small. This makes them feel superior and more powerful. They point the finger of suspicion, blame others, and are hostile to their environment. They make it a point to find the famous "fly in the ointment" and to denounce it with inner satisfaction. The principle of "attack is the best form of defence" applies to the aggressive-devaluing style. Humiliating and oppressing the other person serves an important purpose. It is a shield, so to speak, used to protect the vulnerable within. If there is any danger of being hurt in a certain environment or by any person present, the aggressive-devaluating person blocks all other people from the outset in a brute way. People feel attacked by them and for their part react reservedly and coldly or even aggressively. This behaviour, in turn, confirms one's mistrust and the need to forestall personal injury through one's offensive behaviour.

The messages are crystal clear. On the self-revelation side, it is sent verbally and non-verbally that the aggressive-devaluating person is superior and invincible. On the appeal side, the expectation is that the other person will submit and acknowledge their superiority. In this expectation, the relational side expresses how the other is or should be, namely small, pathetic, to blame for everything, and worth nothing. If two people meet in an aggressive-devaluing communication style, an escalating power struggle breaks out. This does not have to express itself in physical violence. The mutual insults, which are exchanged non-verbally and between the lines, do not lead to bleeding wounds, but the mental wounds are similarly painful. Since neither can back down without acknowledging defeat, such encounters often escalate to the point where the only way to settle the disagreement is to call upon a superior with joint line management responsibility to put their foot down.

- **Proving Communication Style – "Look What I Can Do!"**

For some people, every other person or at least every little familiar person is a judge or rival. Since they pass their judgement, the proof to be without faults and blemishes must be given at any time and over and over again. In an attempt to proof that the person is good and lovable, they use to emphasise their "heroic deeds" and what they have already achieved. This does not have to be done explicitly but can also be done under the guise of being mentioned in passing. For example, this person happened to meet and have animated exchanges with important people, authored something that was even cited multiple times, or they serve on countless important committees and councils. Communication is about their importance and that what is said deserves the recognition of the communication partner - the hook is rather secondary. The insecure and what they perceive as their unlovable side remains hidden deep inside.

The self-revelation is bursting with hints of one's own faultlessness and flawlessness. The appeal side is equally clear: "Give me your approval!" On the relationship side, the expectation to be judged by the interlocutor is conveyed. The attitude can be compared to a judge passing judgment from on high, or a rival competing with one. The urge to appear perfect and to be judged as such puts considerable pressure on the person proving themselves, which is temporarily relieved in situations of success. However, the doubts about themselves remain, so that a little later the proof has to be given again.

- **Determining-Controlling Communication Style – "This Is Allowed and That Is Forbidden"**

A deep-rooted fear of chaos, change and the unknown is countered by people with a controlling style of communication. With their rules, norms and principles, which appear compulsive to other people, these people protect themselves from the agonising feeling of loss of control. Therefore, they meticulously plan their daily routines or develop and pedantically observe rituals. Other people become the source of unpredictability and change. To counter these dangers, others are told exactly how to do something right and even more so how to be right. Letting other people get close to oneself carries the risk of being hurt by them. Therefore, a person reveals as little of themselves and their inner self as possible. I-messages, which reveal something about a person themselves, become the said rules and norms, which are given to people by a higher order, so to speak. So it is said in the direction of another person in the subway in a determining-controlling style "Loud music is forbidden in the subway" instead of revealing oneself with "Your loud music in the headphones disturbs me. Please turn them down a bit". The central self-revelation message in the determining-controlling style is "I know what's right here and now". The appeal side is correspondingly impersonal, filled with messages about how something is wrong or right. On the relational level, communication partners are more or less incapacitated, since they are constantly in danger of doing something wrong and therefore everything has to be explained to them in detail.

- **Distancing Communication Style – "Keep Your Distance"**

Keeping other people at a distance is the basic need of the person communicating in a distancing style. The proper safe distance to other people must always and in every situation be maintained. An aura of aloofness and (emotional) coldness surrounds such a person. To get close to such people or even to experience a feeling of sympathy seems impossible. The distancing person is matter-of-fact and adult in all respects. Surges of emotion in other people are analysed and finally rationalised. This level of attention and consolation should be enough according to the distancing person. The only things that matter are the facts. These are enumerated and evaluated so that rational decisions can be derived.

The self-revelation side expresses that it is none of the other person's business how I am or what is going on inside me. More specifically, the message is, "Nothing is going on inside me." "Keep your distance!" is a clear appeal, delivered through all sorts of nonverbal signals. An arrogant sideways glance, a turned-up nose, and a mild but deprecating smile speak volumes in this context. The relationship message is aimed at denouncing and not allowing what is perceived as far too much emotionality from the other person. Really arguing so that the sparks fly does not work at all in the distancing style. Even the attempt at belligerent resistance is dismissed as unobjective and childish. In a superior pose, the distancing person withdraws and puts distance between themselves and the other person until the latter, according to their definition, behaves like an adult again.

- ■ **Communicative-Dramatic Communication Style – "Attention At Any Cost"**

Communicative-dramatic people are very sociable, as they need their audience to be the centre of attention and to tell the world all sorts of things about themselves. "Attention at all costs" could be the motto. For other people, the experience of talking to such a person can be very entertaining. It is important for them to be noticed and to receive feedback that they are being noticed and taken care of. Self-disclosure and self-revelation are the focus of this communication style. For the partner this means, above all, to take up the smorgasbord of messages and to confirm how extremely interesting all this is for them. Of course, the richness of detail even in the most intimate stories could lead to the feeling of closeness. But quite soon the impression emerges that it does not really matter who is listening to the communicative-dramatic person. The question also arises as to whom they are actually speaking. After all, their extroverted behaviour is based on the desire to feel themselves by telling others about themselves. The more special and unusual the respective story is for the listener(s), the more the speaker can feel that they are being noticed and are really there.

As said before: The self-revelation side is wide open and pretty much everything is revealed without reflection. The goal is to excite the audience. The simultaneous appeal is, "Listen to me and validate me or validate my self-presentation!" The relationship side is ambiguous. On the one hand, the other person is really important to the communicative dramatist(s). Unfortunately, the importance does not result from the person being interchangeable. The other person is important as an audience, as a listener in itself. The best audience signals how rushing and how special the other person's life is perceived to be. The other extreme can also be served. The extensive report about one's strokes of fate or other threatening developments, such as illnesses often exerts a similar fascination as success stories.

> **Reflection task: Personal experiences with communication styles**
> Please recall your last five conversational situations. In what style did you communicate and how did the people you talked to communicate? Can you identify a pattern in communication style for you or the other people?

3.2 Tools and Instruments for the Study of Communication

By now we have learned a lot of basic things about human communication. Life offers an infinite abundance of encounters with other people, which - as we keep emphasising - also involve communication. The division into communication styles and their examination by means of the four sides of a message is an important tool (toolbox) for examining concrete communication situations.

> **Toolbox**
> In the following, we would like to present further tools and instruments by which communication can be analysed in more detail:
> - (Vicious) circles in communication
> - The values and development square
> - The drama triangle
>
> Think of this chapter as a **toolbox**. You can use these tools and instruments to analyse and examine communication as well as communication breakdowns. In addition, they open up the possibility of adapting your communication in a targeted manner.

3.2.1 (Vicious) Circles in Communication

Communication is circular. There is neither a starting point nor an endpoint. The person takes in what they receive from other people and process what they have received. Then the person reacts, and it is the other person's turn (Schulz von Thun, 2013; Watzlawick et al., 1968). To illustrate the processes, Schulz von Thun uses a circuit diagram from systems therapy (Thomann & Schulz von Thun, 2005).

To explain the scheme in ◘ Fig. 3.2, let us start the communication process with person A. Person A expresses himself with actions or reactions (1), person B reacts inwardly with feelings and sensations to what person A has expressed (4) and expresses himself in turn (2), person A reacts inwardly to what person B has expressed (3) and expresses himself again (1), and so on. Often there are so-called **auxiliary motors** (5 and 6) on both sides, which additionally intensify the feelings and sensations. Only the respective expressions (2 and 4) are observable for both; what happens inside one person remains hidden from the other.

> ▶ **Case Study**
>
> Let us look again at an example from everyday work. Mr Wilson - you have already met him in a previous example - usually behaves rigidly, unyieldingly and controllingly towards a trainee. He frequently accuses him of being unpunctual and of constantly

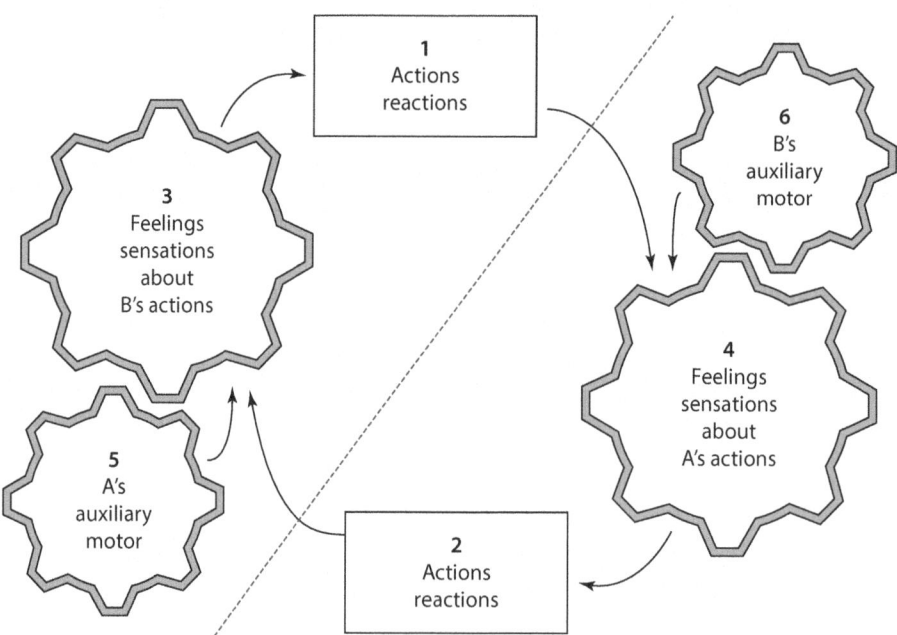

◘ **Fig. 3.2** Interpersonal circuit diagram ("vicious circle"). The figure shows a cycle of communication between two people A and B. Statements made by an interlocutor (actions/reactions) activate feelings and sensations in the other interlocutor, who in turn responds with actions and reactions, thereby triggering feelings and sensations in person A. (Source: Own representation based on Thomann and Schulz von Thun, 2005, p. 327)

3.2 · Tools and Instruments for the Study of Communication

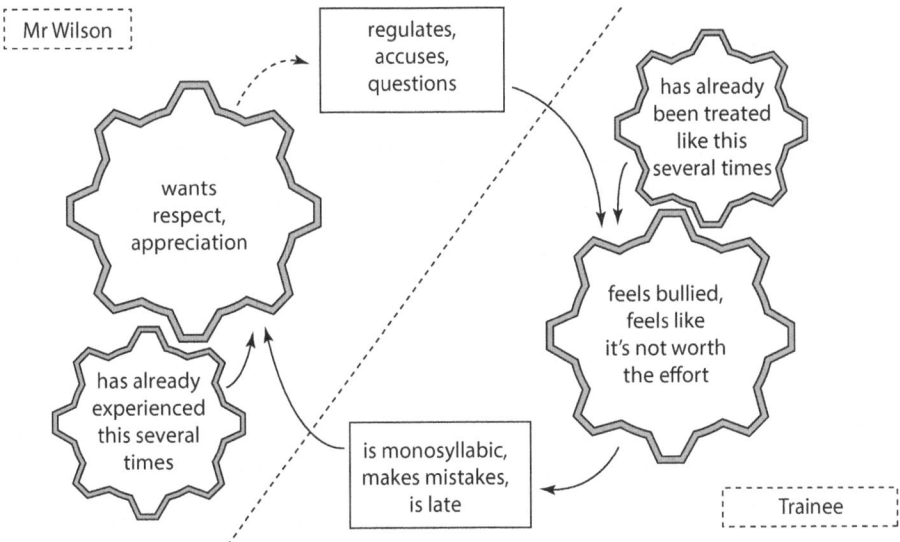

Fig. 3.3 Vicious circle using the example of Mr. Wilson and the trainee. With the help of such a cycle model (shown here using the example of Mr. Wilson and the trainee), communication disorders can be examined and they are helpful in reflecting on one's communication behaviour. (Source: Own representation based on Thomann and Schulz von Thun, 2005, p. 327)

making mistakes. This interaction between Mr Wilson and the trainee is observable for both of them and also for an outsider. Inwardly, the trainee feels immature and controlled. Everything he does is controlled and criticised by Mr Wilson anyway. Why should he make any effort? Now to the inside of Mr Wilson: Mr Wilson wants to be respected and make a good impression, especially on his manager. Therefore, he acts in an authoritarian manner and meticulously controls his employees. This is reinforced by the fact that both Mr Wilson and the trainee have already clashed frequently. All in all, a classic vicious circle (see Fig. 3.3). ◀

The preceding example shows that it does not make sense to divide communication into categories such as "malicious", "sick" or "immature". The communicative system in the example is very stable and the participants behave comprehensibly against the background of their respective realities. Therefore, it is worthwhile to look for such constellations when communication is disturbed, for example in conflicts. If these are made visible (e.g. in early conflict phases through the use of a moderator), there is a chance of resolving them (Schulz von Thun, 2008).

If communication is cyclical, does this not raise the question of the extent to which the person being addressed had themselves helped to put a communicative bait on the hook? For this purpose, let us take another closer look at some communication styles - following Schulz von Thun (2008). Let us take a person who wants to feel stronger and superior. If this person is addressed in the needy-dependent style, the feeling of superiority is strengthened in them. They might respond by taking on a task that is unmanageable for the other person. They say and think, "I'll do it!". The other person feels validated in their need for help and continues to send their basic message, "I can't do it. Please help me!", so closing the circle.

Another person may feel the need to separate themselves and not even "give an inch" to the other person who is obviously in need of help. They feel harassed and fear being taken advantage of. They will refuse any assistance and say, "Leave me alone. Do it yourself". The other person will then feel left alone and not loved, just pathetic. They will increase their efforts to get help, keep persisting and asking or begging for help. This also closes the circle.

What does it all look like with the helping communication style? A person wants to feel independent and superior. Therefore, they emphatically offer their advice and help to other people. If the person addressed already feels in need of help, this feeling is confirmed and they willingly accept the help. This closes the circle.

The interaction of needy-dependent and helping communication style can also develop in another direction. The feeling of dependence on the part of the person in need of help can be supplemented by a feeling of humiliation (the helper knows and can do everything better and shows it), which can lead to defiance. In this case, it can be signalled that all advice and offers of help are gratefully accepted, but are of no use. The helper feels more and more frustrated, which leads to ever new and ever more irritating advice. The irritated advice is answered again and again with a defiant reaction, in keeping with the motto "I need help and can't do it all alone. But in return I'll prove to you that you don't know any better and can't help me either".

A very stable interaction occurs when the selfless communicator meets someone who wants to feel superior and elevated. The crouched appearance of the selfless person sends exactly this message ("I am smaller than you. Please let me look up to you."), which the superior person wants to hear and feel. They show their benevolent side so that the selfless one feels affirmed and so secure. They want to keep this security at all costs and continue to make themselves small. As long as the superior partner is willing to interact with a person whom they do not experience as an equal, the system remains stable. However, if they begin to long for an equal partner, they may develop a sense of contempt. This manifests itself in further humiliating the self-deprecating person. They, in turn, feel vindicated in their nothingness and keep their head down. Because this is difficult for them to bear, they at the same time signal their moral superiority, since, although they are already "wallowing in the dust", they are nevertheless being kicked. This message can trigger anger or even disgust in those who feel superior, which translates into further humiliation - a true escalating vicious circle. Again, we see that pairs of terms, such as "guilty - innocent" or even "right-wrong" cannot be clearly assigned to the parties involved. Both have their shares and derive some personal benefit from the interaction.

> **Reflection task: Breaking my vicious circle**
> When you think about yourself and other people in your life with the knowledge of vicious circles in communication, can you think of such vicious circles? Please draw the vicious circle in the form shown. How could the vicious circle be broken?

3.2 · Tools and Instruments for the Study of Communication

3.2.2 Values and Development Square

Based on the "Values Square" by Paul Helwig (1965, p. 65), Schulz von Thun has developed the "Values and Development Square" (Schulz von Thun, 2008) (see ◘ Fig. 3.4). This model is based on the premise that a value can only develop its positive effect if it is in positive tension with its positive counter value. "Frugality and generosity" or "trust and prudence" are examples of such pairs. If such a positive relationship of tension does not exist (e.g. a person who is exclusively frugal or who places trust in everything and everyone), the values degenerate into their devaluing exaggerations. Frugality becomes stinginess and trust becomes naive trustfulness (see ◘ Fig. 3.5). Conversely, the same would occur with the positive

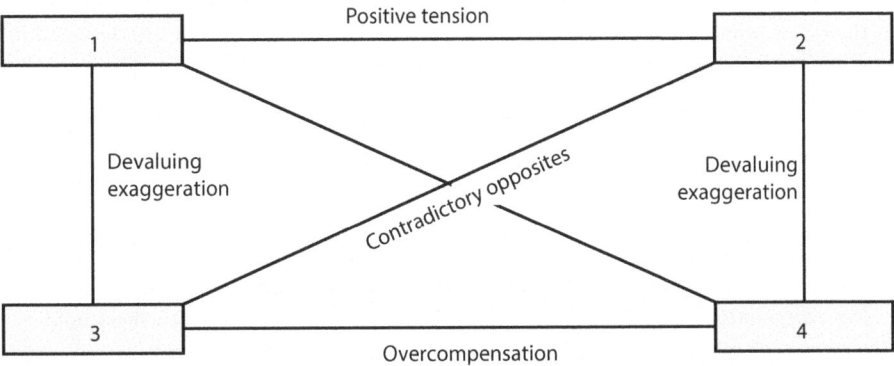

◘ **Fig. 3.4** The Values and Development Square. With the help of the Values and Development Square, Schulz von Thun examines the communication styles he describes in more detail (see ► Sect. 3.1). (Source: Own representation based on Schulz von Thun, 2008, p. 39)

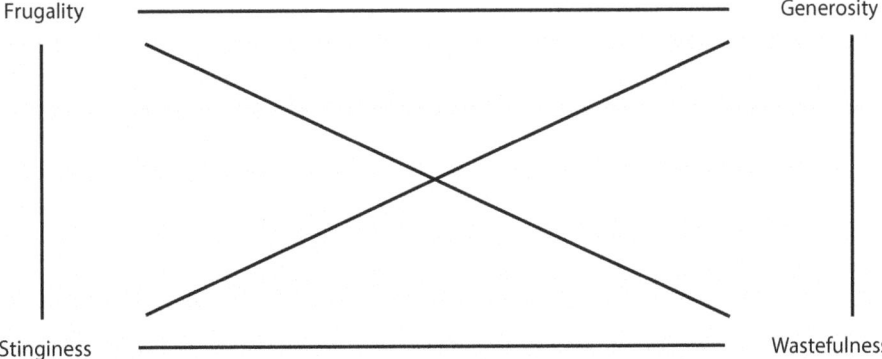

◘ **Fig. 3.5** The Values and Development Square for "frugality - generosity". In the example, the values of frugality and generosity are in a positive relationship of tension. The devaluing exaggerations to these values are stinginess and wastefulness. In other words, excessive frugality leads to stinginess and excessive generosity leads to wastefulness. If a person is excessively frugal, i.e. stingy, the sensible direction of development would be on the diagonal, i.e. towards more generosity. The stingy part would inevitably become smaller in this direction of development and would so develop towards frugality. There would be a chance that the positive tension between frugality and generosity would re-establish. (Source: Own representation based on Schulz von Thun, 2008, p. 39)

counter value. The devaluing exaggerations for generosity and prudence would be wastefulness and paranoid distrust, respectively. The relationship between a value and the devaluing exaggeration of its positive counter value is called a contrary opposition (Helwig, 1965; Schulz von Thun, 2008).

This model opens up the possibility of not perceiving devaluing exaggerations as something bad or even unhealthy, but of returning them to their positive initial value. The positive counter value can then be used to work towards creating a positive tension relationship. The danger is great in such constellations that work is not done on the positive counter value, but the devaluing exaggeration of the positive counter value. In this way, a devaluing counter value could be overcompensated in another devaluing counter value. To take up the example given earlier: If a person is stingy, it would not be purposeful to be wasteful with money in the future. It would, on the other hand, be helpful to be aware of the positive values that are depicted in the upper area of the figure. In this way, there is a chance to be more generous in the future, but not to neglect the positive initial value of stinginess - frugality.

In his book "Talking to each other 2" ("Miteinander Reden 2") Schulz von Thun points out further important value and development squares (Schulz von Thun, 2008).

> **Reflection task: Value and development Squares in political talk shows**
> Please watch the next political talk show considering the question, which devaluing exaggerations the participants (preferably from different political wings) hold against each other. Which values are in positive tension with each other?

> ▶ **Example: Value and Development Square in the Refugee Discussion**
> In discussions, such constellations often lead, consciously or unconsciously, to the polarisation of the positions of the interlocutors. Let us take the current discussion on the reception of refugees in Germany in the period shortly before the writing of this book in 2016. A pair of accusations that repeatedly arise in discussions between different camps can be characterised as follows: One camp is **naively altruistic** and **allows itself to be exploited**, while the other camp is **cold-hearted, egoistic** and **unrelenting** about people's neediness. The camps are arguing at the level of invalidating exaggerations. This dispute is unlikely to lead to an amicable resolution unless some power entity determines how it should be done. If we look at this pairing in the square of values and development, a positive value to naive altruism would be "compassionate helpfulness" and to cold-hearted egoism, it would be "carefully considered pursue of one's own interests". On this basis - without any guarantee of success, of course - the line of compromise could be explored that one camp retains its helpfulness but also formulates and protects its interests, and the other camp in future protects its interests in a balanced way and activates its compassionate and helpful side (◘ Fig. 3.6). ◀

> **Important**
> We are aware that reality is more complex and cannot be reduced only to the pairs of terms mentioned. Please consider the example as an approach from which perhaps a more objective and less polarised discussion becomes possible.

3.2 · Tools and Instruments for the Study of Communication

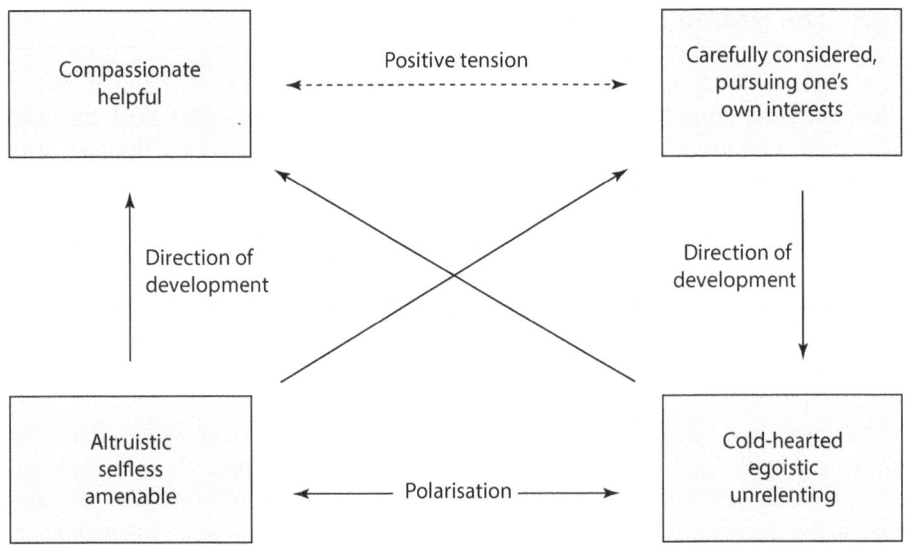

Fig. 3.6 The Values and Development Square for the example of the "refugee discussion". The respective development direction of the two camps lies on the respective diagonal. The objective here is the positive tension between the values "compassionate, helpful" and "carefully considered, pursuing one's own interests". (Source: Own representation based on Schulz von Thun, 2008)

Following Schulz von Thun, let us look at some communication styles with the help of the Values and Development Square (Schulz von Thun, 2008). The person communicating in the needy-dependent style denies their ability to help themselves to an exaggerated degree. But no human being can always and in every situation do without the help of others. Therefore, a positive value, or its non-exaggerated form, would be to be aware that I too am needy and may show weakness. The positive counter value would be to be aware that I am capable of action and responsible for myself. Moving toward this positive counter value could create the positive tension between "asking for and accepting help" and "acting autonomously". It would not be a sensible option to substitute the complete denial of one's own ability to act for the complete denial of one's own need for help.

A person who consistently denies their neediness (as in the helping communication style) exaggerates the positive value of "autonomy" and "responsibility" for their own life. The positive counter value to "autonomy" and "responsibility" would be "the conscious acceptance of one's weaknesses and neediness". In this constellation, a positive tension can arise in which the human being thinks and acts autonomously within the framework of their possibilities but is aware of their needy sides and allows help there.

? Reflection task: Creation of Value and Development Squares
Please develop Value and Development Squares for other communication styles as examples.

3.2.3 The Drama Triangle

In ▶ Sect. 2.4 we looked at transactional analysis according to Eric Berne (1961, 1966) and three core elements (ego states, transactions, views of life). With the help of these three core elements, recurring patterns in human communication can also be systematically examined.

One such communication pattern is **drama**. Imagine a scene in a television soap opera. People are talking to each other, it becomes more and more dramatic, emotions boil up, maybe tears flow or some other kind of emotional outburst occurs. The protagonists get along again, only to plunge into the next drama right after that, and so on. As a viewer, you are sometimes more or less touched, because you have experienced how two people have turned to each other very intensively.

We often ask ourselves about the actual goal of the conversation or how it turned out in the end. Let us take a look at ourselves and see if there are similar encounters as well. To anticipate it: If you answer the question about such encounters in the negative, that would be very unusual. Conversations with people in which we ask ourselves during or afterwards "What is or was the conversation actually about?" occur with every person. There was a lot of talking, feelings - often negative or unpleasant - arose in us, the encounter was very intense and at the end, there is no real result. Please do not be concerned - such a pattern of communication is very human and every human being experiences it in many different forms again and again in their life. There are even relationships between people in which this form of communication takes place almost exclusively.

In transactional analysis, the so-called **drama triangle** is used to approach such communication patterns. In the drama triangle, people with different views of life in different ego states interact primarily with parallel transactions. The last point explains why this form of communication is so stable: All participants experience the interaction as they consciously or unconsciously expect it to be. Now, we might think that it should be a positive sign if people communicate stably with each other. However, the attribute stable says nothing about what content is exchanged and what feelings are involved. In the drama triangle, primarily negative feelings are involved and communication is consistently characterised by mutual devaluation. We can also say that the drama triangle is a very intense form of attention towards each other but in a negative form.

It is precisely the aspect of attention that plays a role in those relationships in which the drama triangle is part of the standard repertoire of interaction. It is often the only way in which people can make contact with each other. Since humans are dependent on attention, negative attention - pejorative interaction - is experienced in the sense that this form of attention is still better than no attention at all (Gührs & Nowak, 2014).

Let us now take a closer look at the drama triangle with the transactional analytic knowledge we have gained so far. In doing so, we will be guided by the explanations of Gührs and Nowak (2014, ◘ Fig. 3.7).

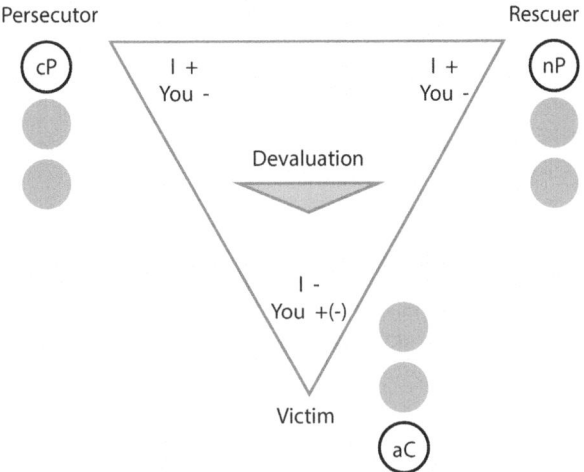

Fig. 3.7 The drama triangle. The drama triangle is another instrument of transactional analysis that can be used to describe and analyse unproductive communication patterns in more detail. This opens up the opportunity to actively change such a communication pattern. (Source: Own representation based on Gührs and Nowak, 2014, p. 121)

In the drama triangle, there are persecutors, sometimes called perpetrators, as well as rescuers and victims. Let us take a closer look at these three "players" or "roles":

1. The **persecutor** has a life view of "I'm okay, you're not okay". The persecutor wants others to feel this sense of superiority. To do this, they energise their critical-normative parent ego - expecting an adapted childhood ego to respond to them. The persecutor is in attack mode, so to speak, and wants to explain to the other person pointing the finger at them what is wrong with them and what failures they are blamed for.
2. The **rescuer** has the same view of life as the persecutor. They, too, see themselves as okay and the other person as not okay. Unlike the persecutor, the rescuer energises their nurturing parent ego in such a way that others appear to be dependent and in need of their help. The rescuer signals to their counterpart, "Without my help you are nothing. Let me help you or do something for you".
3. The **victim** forms the third corner of the drama triangle. Without the victim, the drama triangle cannot be closed. The victim has the life view "I'm not o.k., you're o.k." The victim feels that they are doing everything wrong, worse, that they themselves are wrong. It communicates in the adapted childhood ego. They want to be confirmed that they are wrong and to be told what is right.

Now, different constellations of the drama triangle are conceivable. There is always a victim involved and on the other side a persecutor or a rescuer. Of course, all three positions can also be occupied. The entry into the drama triangle can be made from any position. Let us think of this entry as an invitation or even a trap. Only when another person accepts the invitation or takes the bait, they enter the drama triangle. Again at this point: it does not make any sense to finger point at anyone in a communication process. Everyone is involved in everything that happens - an invitation does not have to be accepted or a bait taken.

Invitations to the drama triangle often begin with exaggerations or generalisations. Words such as "never," "always," "anyone/everyone," "all," etc. are indicative of such an invitation. Here are some examples:
1. "You're always late."
2. "I never do anything right." or "I always do everything wrong."
3. "You never listen to me."
4. "Leave it, as always it's better if I do this for you."

▶ Falling Game

Perhaps you have already experienced the following conversation in a similar form. Imagine a breakfast scene at the Wilsons' involving Mr Wilson, his wife, and his son Tommy.

Mr Wilson:	"Your room looks like a mess again. You never clean up!"

Kevin winces.

Mr Wilson:	"I'm going to say this for the last time. Clean up!"
Mrs Wilson:	"Have you ever taken a closer look at your hobby shed? You can't put one foot in front of the other there either."

Mr Wilson looks puzzled and remains silent.

Tommy:	"Don't bother, Dad's right after all."

A little later, *Mrs Wilson* says to Tommy, "That was the last time I helped you. You always stab me in the back."

Whether Tommy accepts this renewed invitation into the drama triangle remains unknown. The interaction of the three people involved is interesting: Mr Wilson first invites Tommy into the drama triangle as the persecutor. Tommy takes the bait and moves into the role of the victim. Mrs Wilson comes to her son's rescue as the rescuer. Tommy leaves the victim role and becomes a rescuer himself. Finally, Mrs Wilson, as the persecutor, throws out her bait. If Tommy takes this bait, the drama takes its course again … ◀

❓ Reflection task: Drama triangles in TV shows

One way to visualise what you have just learned is to watch a daily soap or telenovela and follow the dialogue of the actors and actresses. If this is not for you, please try to recall your own experiences with the drama triangle. Who played which role in the constellation?

In this form of interaction, the relationship between the participants takes centre stage. The three people turn to each other, define their relationship - each from their point of view - and get a reaction to it. Quite a lot happens, but no result is achieved on the factual level (Gührs & Nowak, 2014).

Was it really about an untidy room or a messy hobby shed? Probably not. If it had been about that, it would have been more purposeful to energise the adult ego. You probably can come up with some criteria for states of tidiness and disorder, so it is possible to have a factual and rational discussion about it. In our experience, the realisation that it is not about the factual content at that moment in the conversation offers the opportunity to consciously avoid the drama triangle and to communicate with each other in a matter-of-fact, appreciative manner.

As long as there is parallel interaction in the drama triangle, communication is stable. The ego states meet as the participants believe they should (Berne, 1961, 1966). With one or more crossed transactions, there is a chance to reject invitations into the drama triangle (Gührs & Nowak, 2014).

► **Case Study**

Since in the case of the drama triangle the parent and childhood ego are involved, crossing with the adult ego is promising. Let us consider the following exemplary situation:

Ms Miller also gets angry sometimes. Especially in the presence of Ms Robinson, who has been getting on her nerves for some time.

Ms Miller (angrily):	"You always leave the door open. There's a draught!"
Ms Robinson (matter-of-factly):	"'Always' is probably an exaggeration. Today, for example, was the first time."

Ms Miller looks irritated.

Ms Robinson:	"Shall I close the door?"
Ms Miller (more quietly):	"Yes, please."

◄

Do not be discouraged if the crossed transaction does not immediately show its effect. Your counterpart may have a deep need to go into the drama triangle. Stay in the adult ego and try again. If you are thinking about moving into the critical-normative parent ego yourself, that is, responding symmetrically, this is a parallel transaction. The conflict stabilises and is likely to escalate further.

Eric Berne has dealt with further patterns of human communication. He speaks in this context of "Games People Play" (Berne, 1966). Sometimes these games are simply about passing the time. For example, people happen to chat about the weather or the youth of today, and agree or disagree. Eventually, people part ways and nothing has changed. But often there are manipulative intentions behind the games and one player wants to gain a benefit from the game at the expense of the other. This benefit is closely related to one's views of life or other beliefs (Berne, 1966).

At this point, we would like to refer to a game that you have certainly already experienced in various forms: The "yes-but-game". The inviter is deeply convinced that a problem or a situation cannot be solved. Their conviction is so deep that the unsolvability also applies to everyone else. With the "yes-but-game", the player wants to prove the unsolvability and so trigger a feeling of triumph in themselves. To do this, it is necessary to frustrate or annoy the other player(s). The player sees themselves overwhelmed and proves the correctness of this feeling by showing that the others are also not able to solve the problem.

A common opening of this game is some form of complaint, combined with an overt or covert request for advice: "What am I supposed to do if …?" (Gührs & Nowak, 2014). The yes-but-player looks for a saviour who will take his bait. Once the rescuer is found, the rescuer will start giving advice. The yes-but-player's response to each piece of advice is a covert patronising "Yes (thank you for your advice), …" coupled with a reason "… but" explaining why this advice is not purposeful. The rescuer is covertly asked to give new advice. The rescuer continues and repeatedly receives the feedback "Yes, but …", which initially causes irritation, then resignation and later often anger. So such a game often ends something like this:

- *Rescuer* (resignedly): "I guess there's nothing to be done."
- *Yes-but-player* (triumphantly): "Yes, but thank you for trying."

Or

- *Saviour* (angry): "You're beyond help!"
- *Yes-but-player* (disappointed, but confirmed): "That's what I said. First, you can't help me and now you reproach me for it."

This closes the circle. The yes-but-player got what they wanted, leaving behind frustrated or even angry teammates.

If you meet a yes-but-player, it is best not to give them any advice at all. Any advice would only fuel the game. Instead, invite them to change their perspective or ask them about their previous approaches to solving the problem. The ego state of choice is the adult ego (Gührs & Nowak, 2014).

> **Reflection task: Stories from the drama triangle**
> Please find more examples of ways to play the drama triangle. Suggestions can be found in the book "Games People Play" (Berne, 1966).

> **Summary in Key Terms**
> - The **eight communication styles** according to Schulz von Thun (2008) demonstrate the dependence of human communication on the inner state of a person.
>   - A distinction is made between the needy-dependent style, the helping style, the selfless style, the aggressive-devaluing style, the determining-controlling style, the distancing and the communicative-dramatic style.
>   - Communication style expresses how a person feels, how they want to appear to others, and how they view their respective relationships with others.
>   - Different people's communication styles harmonise differently when talking to each other.

- The use of various **tools** or instruments facilitates the classification and understanding of communication styles. This includes, for example, the uncovering of vicious circles, the examination of communication-relevant values and principles or even the analysis of a drama triangle.
- Communication is circular. **Vicious circles** in the context of communication arise from the discrepancy between a person's inner attitude and their outer behaviour.
- Excessive **values and principles** can have an escalating effect in interpersonal encounters. With the help of the *Values and Development Square,* exaggerated values and principles can be brought back to their positive initial value.
- Some relationships can be classified in the so-called **drama triangle**, in which the communicating persons behave exclusively pejoratively towards each other.
  - The drama triangle originates from transactional analysis and is based on successful but negative attention of the communicating parties, which is due to different views of life, different ego states but parallel transactions.
  - In a typical drama triangle, three roles can be distinguished: The persecutor, the rescuer and the victim.

Literature

Berne, E. (1961). *Transactional analysis in psychotherapy*. Grove Press.
Berne, E. (1966). *Games people play. The psychology of human relationships*. Deutsch.
Gührs, M., & Nowak, C. (2014). *Das konstruktive Gespräch. Ein Leitfaden für Beratung, Unterricht und Mitarbeiterführung mit Konzepten der Transaktionsanalyse* [The constructive conversation. A guide to coaching, teaching and personnel management involving concepts from transaction analysis] (7th ed.). Christa Limmer.
Helwig, P. (1965). *Charakterologie* [aracterology] (4th ed.). Klett.
Lubienetzki, U., & Schüler-Lubienetzki, H. (2016). *Was wir uns wie sagen und zeigen. Menschliche Kommunikation* [What we say and show to each other and how. Human communication] (study letter of the Fresenius University of Applied Sciences online plus GmbH). Hochschule Fresenius online plus GmbH.
Schulz von Thun, F. (2008). *Miteinander Reden 2 – Stile, Werte und Persönlichkeitsentwicklung* [Talking to one another 2 – Styles, values and personality development] (32th ed.). Rowohlt.
Schulz von Thun, F. (2013). *Miteinander Reden 1 – Störungen und Klärungen* [Talking to one another 1 – Disturbances and clarifications] (50th ed.). Rowohlt.
Thomann, C., & Schulz von Thun, F. (2005). *Klärungshilfe 1 – Handbuch für Therapeuten, Gesprächshelfer und Moderatoren in schwierigen Gesprächen* [Clarification aid 1 – manual for therapists, conversation helpers and facilitators in difficult conversations] (2nd ed.). Rowohlt.
Watzlawick, P., Beavin, J. H., & Jackson, D. D. (1968). *Pragmatics of human communication. A study of interactional patterns, pathologies, and paradoxes*. Faber and Faber.

Disturbed Communication

Sometimes Communication Is Not Successful. But Why Is That?

Contents

4.1 Communication Problems – 58

4.2 The 12 Communication Roadblocks According to Thomas Gordon – 61

Literature – 64

The explanations in this chapter are based on the following study brief: Lubienetzki, U. and Schüler-Lubienetzki, H. (2016). WHAT WE SAY AND SHOW EACH OTHER AND HOW. HUMAN COMMUNICATION. Study letter of the Fresenius University of Applied Sciences (Hochschule Fresenius) online plus GmbH. Idstein: Hochschule Fresenius online plus GmbH.

© Springer-Verlag GmbH Germany, part of Springer Nature 2022
U. Lubienetzki, H. Schüler-Lubienetzki, *How We Talk to Each Other - The Messages We Send With Our Words and Body Language*, https://doi.org/10.1007/978-3-662-64437-9_4

When people meet, they communicate. This is inevitable. People communicate verbally or non-verbally. In doing so, they exchange statements and many kinds of messages. Let us now ask ourselves the question: When is communication successful? Or vice versa: What hinders or disturbs success?

After reading this chapter in-depth, you will be able to ...
- Explain **communication disturbances** and explain their possible causes.
- Explain how to **counteract** communication disturbances.
- Reflect the *four pillars of comprehensibility* of messages and the *four levels of depreciation*.
- Explain the background of **communication barriers** and reflect the **12 communication roadblocks** according to Thomas Gordon (1977).

By *success,* we mean that the goal of communication is reached and the intended effect is achieved. Conversely, communication is unsuccessful when the goal of communication and the intended effect is not achieved.

4.1 Communication Problems

We have already learned about the **five axioms of human communication** according to Watzlawick, Beavin, and Jackson (1968) in ▶ Sect. 2.3. Different types of disturbances in communication result from these axioms. Following Watzlawick et al. (1968), let us examine the five axioms in more detail with regard to possible communication disturbances:
1. **"One cannot *not* communicate."**

→ Communicate openly and clearly!

If we are aware of this axiom, we realise that any attempt to avoid communication will fail. It is then generally advisable, even if we do not want to, either to accept offers of communication or to communicate clearly that we do not want to have a conversation. Any other reaction can lead to disturbances, as we will then have to respond in an unclear and misleading way. Therefore, communication disturbances occur when we ignore communication offers, depriciate our counterpart's statements, or reluctantly accept communication.

When we ignore our interlocutors, we pretend to be deaf or unable to speak the other person's language, or we pretend to have some other reason for not being able to communicate. In the latter case, we would have to consider that we are deceiving our counterpart, but at the same time, we know that we are deceiving. This knowledge, in turn, influences our communication. To depreciate the statements of the partner means to do everything to take away their meaning or at least to change it. If we accept the offer of communication reluctantly, we will send the message, if not verbally, then at least nonverbally, that we don't feel comfortable.

4.1 · Communication Problems

2. **"Every communication has a content and a relationship aspect such that the latter classifies the former."**

→ Clarify relationships and communicate appreciatively!

A basic prerequisite for successful communication is that the relationship between two communication partners must not be negative. Conversely, mutual appreciation and trust are the most important characteristics that support the success of communication. The interlocutors must therefore be clear about their relationship. Successful communication, i.e. achieving goals and avoiding disturbances, can consequently only be achieved by those who are in agreement on the content and relationship levels. The axiom even goes so far as to say that if there is agreement on the relationship side, communication can be successful even if there is disagreement on the content side.

Unresolved relationships first require clarification. Accordingly, the interlocutors offer verbal and non-verbal definitions of their relationship. These relationship definitions can be confirmed, rejected or depreciated by the interlocutor.

Negative relationships, i.e. lack of mutual appreciation and trust, disturb communication. Any attempt to simply "leave out" the relationship level is disturbing and doomed to failure. Unclear relationships are also reflected on the content level, which also leads to disturbances.

3. **"The nature of a relationship is contingent upon the punctuation of the communicational sequences between the communicants."**

→ Take into account that communicators influence each other!

With this axiom, Watzlawick et al. refer to the circularity of communication. Successful communication requires that both interlocutors set the same starting point in their communication. If cause and effect are defined differently by the interlocutors, disturbances will occur. The behaviour of the other interlocutor is consciously or unconsciously conditioned by one's own behaviour. If this is disregarded, one's behaviour can put the other person under pressure or even lead to a self-fulfilling prophecy.

4. **"Human beings communicate both digitally and analogically."**

→ Communicate congruently!

In communication, language and behaviour, i.e. verbal and non-verbal forms of expression, are inseparably linked. If both are clear, unambiguous and congruent, the prerequisite for successful communication resulting from this axiom is given. The greater the incongruence, i.e. the (unconscious) behaviour does not match what is said, the greater the disturbances of communication.

5. **"All communicational interchanges are either symmetrical or complementary, depending on whether they are based on equality or difference."**

→ Observe relationships and corresponding expectations!

The definition of a relationship at every moment of interaction determines which reaction is expected from the counterpart and which is not. If the expected does not happen, symmetry leads to escalation and complementarity to paternalism. Both reactions disturb communication in the long term.

In the axioms of Watzlawick et al., the relationship between two partners takes centre stage. For this, Schulz von Thun (2013) has characterised the image of the relationship level lying underneath the factual content level and being, metaphorically speaking, spiked with needles (p. 199). If the stitches become too painful or too numerous, the relationship level must be clarified before further progress can be made on the factual content level.

Not only disagreements on the relationship level can lead to disturbances, but communication disturbances can also result from the format of the content level, the factual message of a statement. In short, the content of a message is heard by the recipient, but its meaning is not understood. While Watzlawick et al. (1968) more or less assume that the content level is comprehensible to the interlocutors, Schulz von Thun explicitly addresses the issue of **comprehensibility**. By this, he means that spoken or written texts should be designed by the sender in such a way that the receiver has the greatest possible chance of understanding them. As we have already seen in ▶ Sect. 2.5, the four pillars of comprehensibility are (Schulz von Thun, 2013, pp. 160–179)
1. the simplicity in the linguistic formulation,
2. the structure of the text,
3. the brevity and conciseness of the message, and
4. additional stimuli or stimulating stylistic devices.

Communication disturbances become particularly evident in contexts in which the joint solution of a problem causes difficulties. At the heart of the matter is the individual evaluation of the problem and the associated circumstances by each participant. In this context, Gührs and Nowak shed light on what Watzlawick et al. (1968) call "disconfirmation" (p. 86) in communication. They substitute the term "disconfirmation" for depreciation (Gührs & Nowak, 2014, p. 161). In goal-oriented communication, it is important that a problem is first recognised and also acknowledged, and in the second step, it is important to jointly search for solutions. Conversely, the depreciation of the problem leads to the impossibility of dealing with it in a promising way. The four **stages of depreciation** are (Gührs & Nowak, 2014):
1. Stage 1: Denial - the problem does not exist.
2. Stage 2: Downsizing - the problem is not so big.
3. Stage 3: Unsolvability - the problem is not solvable.
4. Stage 4: Lack of personal ability - the problem is not solvable for me.

The stages require to be passed through and solved for all sides and only then can the actual solution to the problem be communicated. If statements are recognised that can be assigned to one of the above-mentioned stages, these offer a starting point to lead the communication partner to the solution of the problem. The way to do this is to first raise the awareness of the problem (stages 1 and 2) and then to derive the solvability (stages 3 and 4). Only when the parties involved acknowledge the basic solvability can they constructively and promisingly work on concrete solutions (Gührs & Nowak, 2014).

> **Important**
> In addition, we would like to refer to the drama triangle presented in ▶ Sect. 3.2.3 and other forms of manipulative games. Any form of communication that involves the depreciation of one or more communication partners cannot be equally successful for all participants. Manipulation in any form is, in our view, a massive depreciation of the other, which makes free development and a fact-oriented discussion impossible.

> **Reflection task: Own experiences with communication disturbances**
> Have you experienced such communication disturbances yourself? What did they look like?

4.2 The 12 Communication Roadblocks According to Thomas Gordon

In human communication, there are numerous aspects that we cannot influence. For example, our conversation partner is a black box for us. We do not know what is on the other person's mind and which emotions drive their actions at any point in time. Even if our counterpart expresses themselves, we receive their subjective view but this is evaluated with our subjective view so that the result does not have to correspond to what was originally intended. Our reality is never completely congruent with that of our counterpart (Schulz von Thun, 2013; Watzlawick et al., 1968).

Nevertheless, we can do something ourselves to increase the probability of communication success. We can avoid ourselves being the cause of a communication failure. Thomas Gordon (1977) speaks in this context of "Roadblocks" (p. 60). These are barriers to communication, which cause another person to close off to us and cause an initially productive communication to stall. Communication blocks are to be understood reactively. By this, we mean that one person wants to communicate productively, and the other person reacts in such a way that further communication is blocked.

Let us observe the following conversation in a professional context between the head of the department Ms Baker and her co-worker Ms Evans:

> ▶ **Example: Joint Problem Solving and Communication Blocks**
> Ms Evans has just returned from an important customer visit.

Ms Evans (matter-of-factly):	"I just went to Lind Company. I tried everything, but they didn't understand me. I've signalled that we're not getting anywhere like this. I'm at my wit's end. What can I do?"
Ms Baker (upset):	"That doesn't sound good. Why didn't you call me right away? I've told you several times."

| Ms Evans (irritated): | "I don't know." |
| Ms Baker (resigned): | "Now I have to fix the situation!" |

Ms Evans is silent.

| Ms Baker: | "I know everything I need to know. You're free to go." |

Ms Evans nods and leaves the room without a word.

In the beginning, Ms. Evans sends the signal that she has got into a situation that does not seem to be solvable for her at the moment. Nevertheless, her will to solve the situation is recognisable. She wants to consult with her supervisor, Ms Baker, in order to prepare a new attempt with the customer. Although Ms Evans has suffered a setback, she still wants to deal with it constructively and opens up to her manager. Ms Baker evaluates what she has heard and responds with a question about why, which simultaneously contains an evaluation as well as an accusation. Ms Evans wanted to look for a solution together and Ms Baker not only does not respond but also evaluates her behaviour negatively and holds it against her. As a reaction, Ms Evans remains silent and so blocks further communication. This leaves Ms Baker with the only option of rectifying the situation herself. Both leave dissatisfied and disappointed. Both of them will think about this incident for some time to come, which means that the communication barrier they have built up will continue to have an effect in the future.

Both, on the other hand, would probably have ended on a positive note if they had had the chance to work together to find a solution that would help Ms Evans solve her problem with the client. They would have had a win-win situation: Ms Evans likely would have returned to her work motivated with the solution to her problem. Ms Baker would have felt a sense of accomplishment with her employee's successful motivation. Ms Evans would have solved the problem herself and Ms Baker would not have had to deal with the problem herself. In the end, the relationship between Ms Baker and Ms Evans would have been strengthened, which would also have improved the chance of working together in a similarly productive manner at the next opportunity. ◀

This was only one way in which a manager can react to an employee and end up alone with the problem. Gordon (1977) lists a total of **12 types of communication roadblocks** (pp. 60–62), sometimes also referred to as the "Dirty Dozen" (Adams, 2012):
1. "Ordering, Directing, Commanding [...]
2. Warning, Admonishing, Threatening [...]
3. Moralizing, Preaching, Imploring [...]
4. Advising, Giving Suggestions or Solutions [...]
5. Persuading with Logic, Lecturing, Arguing [...]
6. Judging, Criticizing, Disagreeing, Blaming [...]
7. Praising, Agreeing, Evaluating Positively, Buttering Up [...]

8. Name-calling, Ridiculing, Shaming [...]
9. Interpreting, Analyzing, Diagnosing [...]
10. Reassuring, Sympathizing, Consoling, Supporting [...]
11. Probing, Questioning, Interrogating [...]
12. Distracting, Diverting, Kidding [...]"

> **Reflection task: Who causes communication barriers?**
> Do you know someone who frequently uses communication blocks? Which ones do they use?

To prevent communication from stalling or breaking down, be sure to avoid the 12 types of communication roadblocks. Instead, you should make use of some techniques to support communication. Often you will get more information if you ask your conversation partner to continue talking ("Would you like to talk about it?") (Gordon, 1977, p. 54). Open-ended questions beginning with "How" might also serve that purpose ("How did it make you feel?").

Such active listening aims to really perceive what the other person wants and to really get in touch. In active listening, we want to hear and understand a statement in all its facets. To do this, the other person must necessarily provide information and underlying messages until we understand the statement. On the other hand, during the conversation, you should make sure that you have correctly understood the diverse information and messages. To do this, repeat important passages in your own words (paraphrasing) and combine this with the question of whether you have understood everything correctly (Gordon, 1977).

> ▶ **Example: Active Listening**
>
> *Ms Baker*: "I understood you said that the Lind company had voiced... and so signalled.... Did I understand you correctly there?"
>
> ◀

In communication, listening well is extremely important. On the one hand, we learn more when we listen well, and on the other hand, we signal to the other person our appreciation of the person and what they are is saying. This behaviour in turn promotes communication.

> **Reflection task: Communication between Ms Baker and Ms Evans**
> Please look again at the conversation between Ms Baker and Ms Evans. How could Ms Baker act or communicate to guide Ms Evans so that she resolves the situation on her own?

> **Summary in Key Terms**
> - **Communication** breakdowns or blocks result in communication being not successful.
> - Possible communication breakdowns can be derived, for example, from the axioms on communication by Watzlawick et al. (1968).

- To counteract communication disturbances or even breakdowns,
    - conversation partners should communicate **clearly** and openly.
    - the communicating parties should clarify their relationship to each other and ensure appreciation as well as trust in the communication process.
    - participants should be aware of the **circularity** of communication, i.e. the conscious and unconscious mutual influence in the communication process.
    - the communicating parties should transmit **congruent** messages.
    - it should be taken into account that **unexpected (re)actions** of the communicating parties can cause disturbances or even disruptions.
- **Communication blocks** occur when a communication partner makes certain statements that lead to a breakdown in communication.
- Thomas Gordon (1977) listed the **12 communication roadblocks**.

Literature

Adams, M. (2012, June 5). *Do you use the dirty dozen when you communicate?* [Blog post]. Retrieved from https://www.gordontraining.com/leadership/do-you-use-the-dirty-dozen-when-you-communicate/

Gordon, T. (1977). *Leader effectiveness training: L.E.T. – The no-lose way to release the productive potential of people* (2nd ed.). Wyden Books.

Gührs, M., & Nowak, C. (2014). *Das konstruktive Gespräch. Ein Leitfaden für Beratung, Unterricht und Mitarbeiterführung mit Konzepten der Transaktionsanalyse* [The constructive conversation. A guide to coaching, teaching and personnel management involving concepts from transaction analysis] (7th ed.). Christa Limmer.

Lubienetzki, U., & Schüler-Lubienetzki, H. (2016). *Was wir uns wie sagen und zeigen. Menschliche Kommunikation* [What we say and show to each other and how. Human communication] (study letter of the Fresenius University of Applied Sciences online plus GmbH). Hochschule Fresenius online plus GmbH.

Schulz von Thun, F. (2013). *Miteinander Reden 1 – Störungen und Klärungen* [Talking to one another 1 – Disturbances and clarifications] (50th ed.). Rowohlt.

Watzlawick, P., Beavin, J. H., & Jackson, D. D. (1968). *Pragmatics of human communication. A study of interactional patterns, pathologies, and paradoxes.* Faber and Faber.

Self-Perception and Perception of Others

What I and Other People Know and Don't Know About Me

Contents

Literature – 68

The explanations in this chapter are based on the following study brief: Lubienetzki, U. and Schüler-Lubienetzki, H. (2016). WHAT WE SAY AND SHOW EACH OTHER AND HOW. HUMAN COMMUNICATION. Study letter of the Fresenius University of Applied Sciences (Hochschule Fresenius) online plus GmbH. Idstein: Hochschule Fresenius online plus GmbH.

© Springer-Verlag GmbH Germany, part of Springer Nature 2022
U. Lubienetzki, H. Schüler-Lubienetzki, *How We Talk to Each Other - The Messages We Send With Our Words and Body Language*, https://doi.org/10.1007/978-3-662-64437-9_5

We have now learned that human communication is significantly more than the spoken word. Language, as we have seen, is only the digital component of communication. People's behaviour and their conscious and unconscious non-verbal signals, such as facial expressions, gestures or body language express much more. This analogic part of communication, through which relationships, feelings and sensitivities are conveyed, dominates the digital part. Or to put it another way: What we communicate through our behaviour is decisive for how others receive what we conveyed verbally.

After reading this chapter in-depth, you will be able to …
- Explain how **self-perception** and the **perception of others** influence communication.
- Explain the **Johari window** as a model for self-perception and perception of others and reproduce the individual cells.
- Derive strategies from the Johari window to increase the chances of successful communication.

What we consciously send depends on our subjective self-perception. When we communicate purposefully, our self-image and our understanding of how we believe others perceive us determine the messages and messages we convey. The receiver, in turn, sees us through subjective "glasses." In doing so, their perception of us only partially coincides with our self-image. Comparable to an iceberg, the largest part of ourselves is hidden from the public. Thus, on the one hand, the other person has a clear information deficit towards us and, at the same time, must evaluate our transmitted digital and analogic signals (Schulz von Thun, 2013; Watzlawick et al., 1968).

This constructivist view of communication has been shaped in particular by Watzlawick et al. and Schulz von Thun (see also ▶ Sect. 2.6). What the other person receives is created in them. In order to put this "puzzle" together, the receiver makes use of their whole personality, their experiences, their perception of their counterpart as well as the semantic content of the messages received (Schulz von Thun, 2013; Watzlawick et al., 1968). Self-perception and perception of others, thus, become a central element of communication: How I perceive myself determines how I communicate. How I am perceived determines what is received.

The model for self-perception and perception of others, originally developed by Joseph Luft and Harry Ingham in the middle of the last century, has now become widely used. The so-called **Johari window** contrasts in a matrix what I do know and what I don't know about myself and what is known and unknown about me to others. Following Gellert and Nowak (2014), the Johari window is structured as follows (see ◘ Fig. 5.1).

This creates four fields or areas:
1. **Secret area**
    The secret area contains everything of mine that is known to me and unknown to others. I decide what becomes public from this area and what is kept confidential.

Self-Perception and Perception of Others

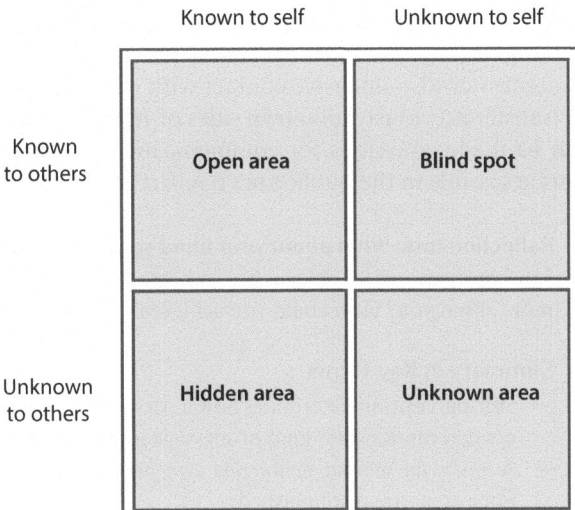

Fig. 5.1 Johari window according to Luft and Ingham. (Source: Own representation based on Gellert and Nowak, 2014, p. 201)

2. **Public area**
   The public area contains everything that I have deliberately made public and that I know others know.
3. **Blind spot**
   My blind spot includes everything that others know about me, but that I know nothing about. The public domain together with the blind spot determines others' perception of me.
4. **Unknown area**
   Much is hidden in the human being, which is unknown to themselves and also to others. Only active work on this area opens up the possibility of learning more about oneself.

In ▶ Chap. 4, we dealt with successful communication. Successful communication is communication that is goal-oriented and actually achieves the goal. In communication relationships (e.g. in the cooperation of groups and teams), success depends on the participants understanding each other. The likelihood of such mutual understanding is greatest when the participants know as much as possible about each other. Thus, group and team collaboration can be improved by increasing the public domain of each individual. There are two basic ways to do this: Mutual feedback and self-disclosure (Gellert & Nowak, 2014).

Mutual feedback causes an individual to become aware of sides previously unknown to themselves. Once the individual is aware of these sides, these become part of the public area. Therefore, all conversation participants are aware of all facts.

Self-revelation makes public what is known to me and what has previously been kept secret from others. In this case, too, mutual communication leads to the desired result that all communication participants become aware of all facts. Before the unknown area can be opened up for conscious communication, targeted self-awareness or also intensive contact with other people is necessary. If it is possible to transfer previously unknown sides of me into the secret area or blind spot, these can be made conscious for communication via self-revelation and feedback and thus accessible in the public area (Gellert & Nowak, 2014).

> **Reflection task: What about your blind spot and public area?**
> In what situations would you like to know more about yourself or wish others knew more about you? How could you achieve the respective goal?

> **Summary in Key Terms**
> - **Self-perception** determines how a person communicates and **perception of others** determines what kind of message is understood by the receiver.
> - A *model for self-perception and perception of others* exists in the **Johari window**. Four areas are distinguished:
> - The **secret area** contains aspects of one's person that are known to oneself and unknown to others.
> - The **public area** contains aspects of your personality and you that are known to you and others.
> - The **blind spot** contains aspects of one's person that are unknown to oneself but known to others.
> - The **unknown area** contains aspects of one's person that are neither known to oneself nor others.
> - To make communication successful, the public domain should be enlarged by reducing the blind spot through **mutual feedback** and the secret domain should be reduced through **self-disclosure**.

Literature

Gellert, M., & Nowak, C. (2014). *Teamarbeit – Teamentwicklung – Teamberatung. Ein Praxisbuch für die Arbeit in und mit Teams* [Teamwork - Team development - Team counselling. A practice book for working in and with teams] (5th ed.). Christa Limmer.

Lubienetzki, U., & Schüler-Lubienetzki, H. (2016). *Was wir uns wie sagen und zeigen. Menschliche Kommunikation* [What we say and show to each other and how. Human communication] (study letter of the Fresenius University of Applied Sciences online plus GmbH). Hochschule Fresenius online plus GmbH.

Schulz von Thun, F. (2013). *Miteinander Reden 1 – Störungen und Klärungen* [Talking to one another 1 – Disturbances and clarifications] (50th ed.). Rowohlt.

Watzlawick, P., Beavin, J. H., & Jackson, D. D. (1968). *Pragmatics of human communication. A study of interactional patterns, pathologies, and paradoxes.* Faber and Faber.

Overall Summary in Keywords

The explanations in this chapter are based on the following study brief: Lubienetzki, U. and Schüler-Lubienetzki, H. (2016). WHAT WE SAY AND SHOW EACH OTHER AND HOW. HUMAN COMMUNICATION. Study letter of the Fresenius University of Applied Sciences (Hochschule Fresenius) online plus GmbH. Idstein: Hochschule Fresenius online plus GmbH.

© Springer-Verlag GmbH Germany, part of Springer Nature 2022
U. Lubienetzki, H. Schüler-Lubienetzki, *How We Talk to Each Other - The Messages We Send With Our Words and Body Language*, https://doi.org/10.1007/978-3-662-64437-9_6

In this book, we have ...
- ... jointly described **human communication** as a verbal or non-verbal interaction between at least two people, analysed it and finally developed our communicative competence.
- ... dealt with different **models, schemes** and **perspectives** on communication, which look at the communicators and the process from different angles with different-sized sections. We have focused on the approaches of *Shannon and Weaver, Watzlawick et al, Schulz von Thun* and *Eric Berne*, among others.
  - Knowledge of these concepts opens up the possibility of directing our view of human communication in different ways and changing it according to our objectives.
- ... with the help of the **first axiom** according to Watzlawick et al. recognised that people who meet inevitably also communicate.
- ... found out that there are several **variables** that influence the interaction of the participants, so the course of human communication is never predictable. These variables include, among others:
  - The **relationship** between the communicating parties, which they may judge differently.
  - The communicating parties themselves in their **inner state**.
  - The respective **context**, but also everything that came before and what will probably be later.
- ... understood with the help of the **second axiom** according to Watzlawick et al. that the *relationship* between communicators has a decisive influence on the meaning of the communicated content.
- ... taken from the **third axiom** according to Watzlawick et al. that communication is *circular*, i.e. virtually without beginning and end.
- ... comprehended on the basis of the **fourth axiom** according to Watzlawick et al. that communication takes place both via the *digital modality*, in the form of what is said or written, and via the *analogic modality,* i.e. via the behaviour, body language and facial expressions of the communicating parties. The digital modality focuses on the factual content and the analogic modality on the relationship aspect.
- ... looked at the **fifth axiom** according to Watzlawick et al., which states that the communication process can be *symmetrical* or *complementary*, depending on whether the relationship between the communicators is based on equality or difference (i.e. relationship or hierarchical gap).
- ... discussed the **four sides of a message** according to Schulz von Thun. According to this, communication takes place on four levels:
  - the *factual content level*,
  - the *relationship level*,
  - the *level of self-revelation,* and
  - the *appeal level*.
- ... summarised, that the **communication style** expresses, among other things, the *inner state* and one's *wishes* for the common relationship as well as for the other person.

6

Overall Summary in Keywords

- ... in the context of communication styles, dealt with various instruments and **tools** for the study of communication:
    - In **vicious circles,** utterances trigger internal emotional reactions, which in turn trigger utterances, and so on.
    - Personal **values** and **principles** as well as a strong desire for attention also determine our communication style.
    - If the need for positive human **attention** is not met, some individuals also accept negative attention and allow themselves to be devalued or demeaned as part of a **drama triangle**.
- ... distinguished **disruptions** and **communication blocks** which can hinder communication from being successful or even prevent it altogether.
- ... presented **measures** to prevent communication disruptions and blocks. The following applies in principle:
    - Notice yourself and others and look out for signs that communication may be disturbed.
    - Always start with yourself first, even though there is a variety of potential causes of communication disturbances because this is the most likely way to bring about change in communication and the behaviour of others.
- ... found out that the course of communication depends decisively on one's behaviour. Therefore, the way we **perceive ourselves** and the knowledge or awareness of how we are **perceived by others** becomes a central element of successful communication.
- ... had a look at self-perception and perception by others which can be examined more closely within the framework of the **Johari window**.

Supplementary Information

Glossary – 74

Index – 77

© Springer-Verlag GmbH Germany, part of Springer Nature 2022
U. Lubienetzki, H. Schüler-Lubienetzki, *How We Talk to Each Other - The Messages We Send With Our Words and Body Language*, https://doi.org/10.1007/978-3-662-64437-9

Glossary

Analogic modality The analogic modality in communication conveys messages through body language in the form of facial expressions, gestures, behaviour, etc., which are usually ambiguous, thus influencing the relationship between communicating parties (Schulz von Thun, 2013; Watzlawick et al., 1968).

Appeal The influence or intention of the sender of a message, which they pursue with their communication and can communicate both covertly and overtly, is called an appeal to the receiver (Schulz von Thun, 2013).

Axiom An axiom is "a statement or principle that is generally accepted to be true, but not need to be so" and might also be "a formal statement or principle in mathematics, science, etc., from which others statements can be obtained" (Cambridge University Press, n.d.).

Communication disturbance If communication is not successful, this is due to a communication disturbance (cf. Watzlawick et al., 1968).

Communication style The term communication style describes a basic pattern that can be observed in human communication (Schulz von Thun, 2008).

Communication roadblock A communication roadblock occurs when one party responds in such a way that further successful communication is not possible (Gordon, 1977).

Congruent message A message is called congruent if all the signals point in the same direction if they are coherent in themselves (Schulz von Thun, 2013, p. 39).

Constructivist A constructivist view in the context of communication means that people first process what reaches them in terms of sensory impressions and then create their subjective reality from this (cf. Schulz von Thun, 2013; Watzlawick et al., 1968).

Digital modality The digital modality in communication primarily conveys factual content and uses language, signs, symbols, etc. to do so (Watzlawick et al., 1968).

Drama triangle In the so-called drama triangle, an instrument of transactional analysis that can be used to describe and analyse unproductive communication patterns in more detail, people with different views of life in different ego states interact primarily via parallel transactions, resulting in intense negative attention (Gührs & Nowak, 2014).

Glossary

Ego state According to Berne (1966), an ego state can "be described phenomenologically as a coherent system of feelings and operationally as a set of coherent behavior patterns" (p. 23).

Human communication Human communication is the verbal or nonverbal interaction between at least two people (Schulz von Thun, 2013; Watzlawick et al., 1968).

Incongruent message A message in which the linguistic and non-linguistic signals do not match is incongruent (Schulz von Thun, 2013, p. 39).

Metacommunication Metacommunication is a conceptual and model system for communicating about communication (Schulz von Thun, 2013; Watzlawick et al., 1968, p. 40).

Perception of others The impressions and beliefs that other people have about one's person can be summarised under the term perception of others (Gellert & Nowak, 2014).

Self-perception Self-perception, as a counterpart to the perception of others, includes all the impressions and beliefs a person has about themselves (Gellert & Nowak, 2014).

Self-revelation or self-disclosure Self-revelation or self-disclosure, whether intended as such or as a natural part of the communication process, reveals information about oneself to others (Schulz von Thun, 2013).

Semantics The term semantics describes "the study of the meanings of words and phrases" (Oxford University Press, n.d.).

Syntax Syntax is "the way in which linguistic elements (such as words) are put together to form constituents (such as phrases or clauses)" (Merriam-Webster, n.d.).

Transaction A transaction is "the unit of social intercourse" (Berne, 1966, p. 29).

View of life A view of life is a person's basic attitude towards their own life and towards relationships with others (Harris, 1969).

Index

A

Adapted childhood ego 19
Adult ego 18
Aggressive-devaluing 40
Analogic modality 15
Analysis 16
Appeal message 30
Auxiliary motors 44
Axiom 9, 13–15

B

Blind spot 67

C

Childhood ego 17, 18
Communication style 38
Communicative-dramatic 42
Complementary 15, 21
Comprehensibility 60
Congruent 30
Constructivist view 33
Covert transaction 25
Critical-normative parent ego 19
Crossed transaction 24

D

Decoding 10
Depreciation 60
Determining-controlling 41
Development 47
Digital modality 15
Dirty Dozen 62
Distancing 42
Drama 50
Drama triangle 50

E

Ego state 17
Emergence 32
Encoding 10
Exaggerations 47

F

Factual content 29
Free childhood ego 18
Functional model of the ego states 18

H

Helping 39

I

Incongruent 30
Invitations 52

J

Johari window 66

M

Metacommunication 10
Mutual feedback 67

N

Needy-dependent 39
Nurturing-caring parent ego 20

O

Okay, views of life 27

P

Parallel transaction 21
Parent ego 18, 19
Persecutor 51
Proving communication 41
Public area 67

Q

Qualification 31

R

Rebellious childhood ego 19
Receiver 10
Relationship 29
Rescuer 51
Roadblocks 62

S

Secret area 66
Selfless 40
Self-revelation 29, 67
Semantics 11
Sender-receiver model 10
Sides 28–30
Square 47
Stimulus 17
Symmetrical 15
Syntax 11

T

Transactional response 16, 17

U

Unknown area 67

V

Values 47
Values and development square 47–49
Vicious circles 44–46
Victim 51
Views of life 26

Y

Yes-but-game 53

The manufacturer's authorised representative in the EU is Springer Nature Customer Service Centre GmbH, Europaplatz 3, 69115 Heidelberg, Germany. If you have any concerns regarding our products, please contact ProductSafety@springernature.com

Printed and bound by CPI Group (UK) Ltd, Croydon, CR0 4YY

23/03/2026

02076398-0013